D0793901

THE
PROJECT
MANAGER'S
PARTNER

Second Edition

THE PROJECT MANAGER'S PARTNER

Second Edition

A Step-by-Step Guide to Project Management

Michael Greer

AMACOM
American Management Association
New York • Atlanta • Brussels • Buenos Aires • Chicago • London • Mexico City
San Francisco • Shanghai • Tokyo • Toronto • Washington, D.C.

Special discounts on bulk quantities of AMACOM books are available to corporations, professional associations, and other organizations. For details, contact Special Sales Department, AMACOM, a division of American Management Association, 1601 Broadway, New York, NY 10019.
Tel.: 212-903-8316. Fax: 212-903-8083.
Web site: www.amacombooks.org

This publication is designed to provide accurate and authoritative information in regard to the subject matter covered. It is sold with the understanding that the publisher is not engaged in rendering legal, accounting, or other professional service. If legal advice or other expert assistance is required, the services of a competent professional person should be sought.

Library of Congress Cataloging-in-Publication Data

Greer, Michael
    The project manager's partner : a step-by-step guide to project management / Michael Greer.—2nd ed.
        p.   cm.
    Includes bibliographical references and index.
    ISBN 0-8144-7133-1
    1. Project management.   I. Title: Step-by-step guide to project management.   II. Title.

HD69.P75   G74   2001
658.4' 04—dc21

2001046069

© 2002 HRD Press.
All rights reserved.
Printed in the United States of America.

This publication may not be reproduced,
stored in a retrieval system,
or transmitted in whole or in part,
in any form or by any means, electronic,
mechanical, photocopying, recording, or otherwise,
without the prior written permission of AMACOM,
a division of American Management Association,
1601 Broadway, New York, NY 10019.

Printing number

10 9 8 7 6 5 4 3 2

For Bonnie, my one true partner in the project of my life

CONTENTS

Acknowledgments   xi

Introduction   1

  Is This Handbook for You?   1
    Some Important Distinctions   2
    Organizational Structures and How They Influence Projects   4
    General Management Skills and the Project Manager   6
  How to Use This Handbook   6
    Part I. Your Deliverables, Phases, and Project Life Cycle   6
    Part II: Your Essential Project Actions   7
    Part III: Your Project Management Action Items   7
  Where to Begin   7

Part I: Your Deliverables, Phases, and Project Life Cycle   9

  Project Deliverables   9
  Project Phases   10
  The Project Life Cycle   11
    Phase I: Determine Need and Feasibility   12
    Phase II: Create the Project Plan   13
    Phase III: Create Deliverables' Specifications   14
    Phase IV: Create Deliverables   15
    Phase V: Test and Implement Deliverables   15
  Assignment: Your Unique Project Life Cycle   16

Part II: Your Essential Project Actions   19

  Project Management Processes   19
    Initiating   20
    Planning   20
    Executing   22
    Controlling   22
    Closing   23

Project Phases and the Project Management Processes   23
Assignment: Your Essential Project Actions   24
Worksheet: Summary of Key Project Manager Actions and Results   24
Phases, Processes, and Action Items: Pulling It All Together   27

Part III: Your Project Management Action Items   29

Overview   29
Initiating   31
   Action Item: Demonstrate Project Need and Feasibility   31
      Worksheet: Demonstrating Project Need and Feasibility   32
   Action Item: Obtain Project Authorization   35
      Worksheet: Is This Project Authorized?   35
      Worksheet: The Project Charter   36
   Action Item: Obtain Authorization for the Phase   39
      Worksheet: Is This Phase Really Authorized?   40
Planning   42
   Action Item: Describe Project Scope   43
      Checklist: Evaluating Project Scope   46
      Worksheet: Project Scope Statement   47
   Action Item: Define and Sequence Project Activities   49
      Guidelines for Defining and Sequencing Project Activities 52
   Action Item: Estimate Durations for Activities and Resources
      Required   55
      Example: Effort/Duration Table   56
      Guidelines for Estimating Durations for Activities and
        Resources Required   58
      Worksheet: Estimating Durations, Resources, and Effort   59
   Action Item: Develop a Project Schedule   62
      Guidelines for Developing the Project Schedule   63
   Action Item: Estimate Costs   70
      Guidelines for Making a Bottom-Up Cost Estimate   72
   Action Item: Build a Budget and Spending Plan   75
      Guidelines for Building a Budget and Spending Plan   75
   Optional Action Item: Create a Formal Quality Plan   78
      Guidelines for Creating a Formal Quality Plan   79
   Optional Action Item: Create a Formal Project Communications
      Plan   81
      Guidelines for Developing the Project Communications Plan 81
      Worksheet: Project Communications Planner   82
   Action Item: Organize and Acquire Staff   85
      Guidelines for Developing the Organizational Plan and
        Strategy for Acquiring Staff   86

Worksheet: Project Responsibility/Accountability Matrix　88
Optional Action Item: Identify Risks and Plan to Respond　91
Guidelines for Identifying Risks and Planning to Respond　92
Worksheet: Risk Assessment and Response Analyzer　93
Optional Action Item: Plan for and Acquire Outside Resources　96
Guidelines for Planning to Procure Outside Goods or Services　97
Guidelines for Soliciting Bids for Outside Goods or Services　99
Guidelines for Selecting the Best Contractor for the Job　100
Action Item: Organize the Project Plan　103
Guidelines for Building the Project Plan　103
Action Item: Close Out the Project Planning Phase　106
Guidelines for Closing Out the Project Planning Phase　106
Action Item: Revisit the Project Plan and Replan if Needed　109
Guidelines for Revisiting the Plan and Replanning if Needed　109
Executing　111
Action Item: Execute Project Activities　112
Guidelines for Executing a Project Phase　112
Guidelines for Recognizing Project Team Members　114
Controlling　117
Action Item: Control Project Activities　118
Guidelines for Controlling a Project Phase　119
Guidelines for Keeping Things Moving: A To-Do List and Items to Help You Execute, Control, and Close Out Your Project　120
Worksheet: Project Deliverables' Status Analyzer　122
Worksheet: Variance Analyzer　123
Guidelines for Handling Scope Change　124
Worksheet: Project Scope Change Order　125
Worksheet: Project Issue Tracker　126
Worksheet: The Project Status Report　127
Closing　129
Action Item: Close Out Project Activities　129
Guidelines for Closing Out a Project Phase　130
Project Postmortem Review Questions　131
Worksheet: Sample Project Sign-Off Form　134

Appendix A: Tips for Managing Experts Outside Your Expertise　**137**

Appendix B: Glossary of Project Management Terms　**141**

Appendix C: Summary of Key Project Manager Actions and Results　**151**

Appendix D: Potential Shortcuts for Low-Risk Projects   155

Appendix E: Guidelines for Deciding When to Kill the Project   159

Appendix F: Taking Charge of Your Project Management Software 161

Appendix G: Selected Project Manager Resources   165

Notes   167

Index   171

About the Author   177

ACKNOWLEDGMENTS

This handbook, like its predecessor, is largely based on the Project Management Institute's (PMI's) *A Guide to the Project Management Body of Knowledge (PMBOK)*, produced by PMI's Standards Committee. Founded in 1969 and representing thousands of full-time project management professionals, PMI has in recent years spent considerable effort in defining and standardizing terms, procedures, and concepts related to the field of project management. Among other services, PMI provides formal testing of those wishing to earn their Project Management Professional (PMP) certification.

Though this handbook is designed primarily for new or part-time project managers who are not likely to seek PMP certification, I felt it extremely important that the terms and concepts presented in this text conform as closely as possible to the standards established by PMI. In this way, users of this handbook may interact more knowledgeably with their PMP-certified colleagues and more effectively use PMI project management references, commercial project management software, and other resources that require knowledge of standard project management terminology and concepts.

In order to remain true to PMI's standardized vision of project management, I have in this handbook generally used the exact definitions of project management terms and the exact descriptions of project management concepts as they are presented in the *PMBOK*. In addition, I have reproduced several graphics directly from the *PMBOK*. I thank PMI for providing the *PMBOK* as a most comprehensive reference and source of inspiration.

In addition, I thank the following reviewers for providing "reality checks" and valuable feedback regarding this handbook during the development of the first edition:

- Valorie Beer, Netscape Communications
- Clyde Bennett, systems engineer
- Cynthia France, The Southern Company
- John Greer, Pennsylvania Electric Co. (ret.)
- Jacqueline Hazlett, AT&T

- Heidi Smith, Apria Healthcare
- Wendy Weeks, Microsoft Corp.
- Karen Wolfe, Xerox Corp.

I thank my many workshop clients and attendees who were both ornery and courageous enough to argue the fine points and demand clarification of parts of the original *Partner*. They forced me to clarify my thinking, and that clarity, I hope, is reflected here.

Finally, to the many hard-working project managers who freely shared their favorite PM items, I say, ''Thank you!'' These real-world contributions are the source of inspiration for most of the new worksheets and checklists that breathe life into this edition.

THE
PROJECT
MANAGER'S
PARTNER

Second Edition

INTRODUCTION

Whether you work in a billion-dollar corporation or a single-person consultancy, sooner or later you are likely to find yourself in charge of a project. The project may be as complicated as the introduction of a whole new product line or as straightforward as moving into a new office. But no matter how simple or complex, you will need to plan and manage your project carefully if you are to achieve high-quality results on time and within budget. Such planning and management can be tough—especially if it's your first time as a project manager.

The good news is that, in recent years, project management has emerged as a distinct profession. That profession has consolidated a set of recommended standards and practices that anyone can learn and implement with any kind of project. By applying the standards and practices to your projects, you can achieve high-quality results while avoiding schedule delays and cost overruns.

The bad news is that it can take considerable time to learn these standards and practices. And in today's downsized, competitive environment, you may not be able to set aside your other job responsibilities to spend time learning all about project management. That's why I've created *The Project Manager's Partner*.

The Project Manager's Partner is a set of items to help project managers ask the right questions and do the right things to get the job done. While it can serve as a valuable quick reference for the experienced project management professional, it is primarily intended to help the new or part-time project manager build a solid foundation of good project management habits.

IS THIS HANDBOOK FOR YOU?

Here are some assumptions I am making about you, the user of this handbook:

- You are responsible for managing a project of some kind.
- You would like your project to achieve quality results, on time and within budget.
- You have training or experience in a particular field such as marketing, engi-

1

neering, accounting, computer installation, desktop publishing, or one of a thousand other specialties.

- You know your profession and you have a pretty good idea of the kinds of results (i.e., the finished product or customer impact) your project should achieve.
- You're not quite sure about all the things you need to do to manage your project.
- You have little or no formal training in project management.
- You are probably serving as project manager at the same time you are making your own contribution to the project as a specialist in your field (i.e., you may be managing the project on a part-time basis).
- You would like to know enough about project management to be able to figure out what a project manager needs to do, with whom, and when.
- You have no need to learn all the sophisticated management techniques that a project manager would need in order to manage a billion-dollar construction project or to land a spacecraft on Mars.
- You or your supervisor recognizes that you need to establish a foundation of basic project management habits that may later be enhanced and adjusted to fit your industry or organization.

If most of the above statements apply to you, then *The Project Manager's Partner* is for you.

SOME IMPORTANT DISTINCTIONS

In this handbook, I am advocating certain actions that can help you become a more effective project manager. Note that I am focusing only on projects and project management. Unfortunately, it's easy to confuse project management–related practices with all sorts of other management practices.

ONGOING OPERATIONS VS. PROJECTS VS. PROGRAMS

Below are some important distinctions to keep in mind.

Ongoing operations are those activities undertaken by an organization routinely and repetitively to generate the goods or services it has been set up to generate.[1] For example, a trucking operation picks up freight, makes deliveries, handles associated paperwork, and so on. These constitute its ongoing operations.

In contrast, *projects* are temporary endeavors undertaken to create a unique product or service.[2] So, for example, when the trucking company decides to build a new warehouse, it is engaged in a project. This project (a temporary endeavor) will eventually come to an end, culminating in a new warehouse that will become part of the company's ongoing operations.

A *program,* on the other hand, is a group of related projects managed together.[3]

Programs usually include an element of ongoing activity. To extend our example, let's say the trucking company has decided that a valuable long-term goal is to expand its operations from handling regional, East Coast freight to handling continent-wide deliveries. It will need to build several more warehouses in order to achieve this goal. In this case, the building of each new warehouse is a *project*. At the same time, the overall expansion effort is a *program* consisting of many projects.

Caution: If you are a new or part-time project manager who also has general management responsibilities in your organization, it's easy to get confused about whether you are managing an ongoing operation, a program, or a project. In particular, a project (a temporary, finite endeavor) demands that you closely monitor the project budget and schedule, take steps to keep things moving, obtain timely approval of deliverables, and attain closure of project phases. Therefore, the actions required to manage a project are sometimes different from those required to manage an ongoing operation or program.

Note that the concept of a project is relative. For example, if you were planning to move your family from one house to another, you would likely view the move as a project. On the other hand, such a move would simply be another part of the ongoing operations of a company in the home moving business.

GENERAL MANAGEMENT VS. PRACTICE OF AN APPLICATION AREA VS. PROJECT MANAGEMENT

General management encompasses planning, organizing, staffing, executing, and controlling the operations of an ongoing enterprise.[4] It is an entire field of study in which people earn advanced degrees and spend years on the job refining their skills. Thousands of books, seminars, and ongoing training programs are available to support people who want to improve their knowledge and skills relating to general management. This handbook does not address general management practices.

Practice of an application area involves those activities typically undertaken by professionals who work in a particular field or industry sector.[5] For example, there are "best practices" or standard operating procedures in the construction industry, the software development industry, the defense industry, and lots of other industries. This handbook does not address specific techniques related to practice of a particular application area.

Project management is the application of knowledge, skills, items, and techniques to project activities in order to meet or exceed stakeholder needs and expectations.[6] This handbook focuses solely on project management practices.

PROJECTS VS. SUBPROJECTS

Projects are often divided into more manageable components called *subprojects*.[7] These may then be contracted out to external vendors or assigned to smaller teams. For example, let's say you have decided to take on the project of remodeling your kitchen. Because you are familiar with painting and enjoy it, you decide to paint the walls yourself. However, because you don't know how to install the tiles for the floor and countertops, you decide to hire a tiling contractor to do this work. In this case, you've divided your overall project (remodeling your kitchen) into two subprojects—painting and tiling.

As a project manager, you must rely on your knowledge of your industry, your available resources, and other considerations to decide when and how to organize your projects into subprojects.

Caution: Subprojects may require separate tracking systems by which the ''owner'' or person responsible for the subproject keeps detailed records of his or her subproject activities. This separate tracking makes it particularly important to establish clear lines of communication between the subproject team and those involved in the larger project of which the subproject is part.

ORGANIZATIONAL STRUCTURES AND HOW THEY INFLUENCE PROJECTS

A project doesn't happen in a vacuum. Projects are nearly always executed by organizations that are larger than the project.[8] These organizations may be set up as companies, agencies, or other institutions. As project manager, you must figure out how to staff your project with specialists from these larger organizations in order to create your project deliverables. In addition, the people who must review and approve your project deliverables (i.e., the sponsors and stakeholders) are also members of larger organizations. They need to be available to make critical interventions (such as review and approve deliverables) exactly when needed. Finally, these organizations provide money to fund the project, equipment for use by the project team, facilities to support project activities, and so on. Unless these organizations make these human and nonhuman resources available when you need them, your project may be difficult or impossible to complete.

For example, if the performing organization has only five computers and ten are required to execute the project, then you will need to rent more computers or lengthen the project schedule. Or if the organization can make available only three engineers and seven are required for the project, then you may need to use an outside contractor to support the project.

Organizational structures are designed in part to control the resources of the organization. For example, a graphic artist who works in the advertising department would likely need to obtain permission from the advertising department manager before participating on your project team. Or if you intend to conduct project team meetings in the company's training department conference center, you may need to obtain permission from the training department manager to schedule the center. In these examples, the department managers (managers of ongoing efforts) are in a position to make or break your project by deciding whether you will get the resources you need in order to complete your project activities.

Organizational structures differ from one organization to another. Some types of organizational structures are specifically designed to support people working on projects, while others are more oriented toward supporting people engaged in ongoing efforts. As project manager, you should be aware of the structure of the organizations from which you must draw your resources. In this way, you can use these structures more effectively.

Note: You might find that experienced project managers or your supervisor might be able to help you identify the ways in which your project is similar to, or different from, projects that the organization has supported in the past. By discussing these similarities and differences with an experienced project veteran, you can figure out how to take full advantage of the organization's resources to support your project.

THE FUNCTIONAL ORGANIZATION

In the *functional organization,* staff are grouped by specialty.[9] For instance, there may be a production department, a marketing department, an engineering department, an accounting department, and so on. While functional organizations perform projects, it is often the case that these projects are limited to the boundaries of the particular function.[10]

For example, let's say a functionally organized computer manufacturer is about to introduce a new computer. In this company, the engineering department might be working on a project to develop a prototype of the new computer, while the marketing department might be working on a separate project to create a marketing plan for the new computer. Each of these "projects" might be more actually described as a subproject of the larger project, which is to introduce the new computer. The manager of the larger project will need to work across the boundaries of the various functional departments in order to get things done. He or she will likely have limited authority and few dedicated resources, since the project team members report to functional department heads.

If your project requires the use of resources from functional organizations, you should plan to spend a significant amount of time and effort in obtaining approval from the managers of the departments from which these resources will be drawn.

THE PROJECTIZED ORGANIZATION

At the other extreme, in a *projectized organization,* staff members are grouped entirely by project and often located physically together.[11] Thus, if our new computer were being introduced by a company that was projectized in its organization, all the project staff members (engineers, marketers, programmers, and so on) might share office space in a separate building. While they may be organized into departments, the departments would be project related. In this case, the project manager could have a high degree of authority over the departments and a substantial amount of resources dedicated to the project.

The Matrix Organization

A *matrix organization* is a blend of the functional and projectized organizations.[12] Typically, the matrix organization is organized by functional departments (like the functional organization), but the project manager usually has his or her own supporting resources and substantially more authority to acquire and manage resources from within each department.[13]

Several gradations of the matrix organization have been identified in PMI's *PMBOK*, including strong matrix, weak matrix, and balanced matrix.

General Management Skills and the Project Manager

There are a number of general management skills that are required of the effective project manager. Addressing all these skills is beyond the scope of this handbook. However, I have identified below the more important skills so that you can decide which you may need to pursue:

- *Ongoing enterprise management skills,* including finance and accounting, sales and marketing, research and development, manufacturing and distribution, strategic planning, tactical planning, organizational behavior, and managing relationships.[14]
- *General management* skills likely to affect most projects:[15]
  —Leading (leadership)
  —Communicating
  —Negotiating
  —Problem solving
  —Influencing the organization

If you need improvement in any of these general management skills, you should consider obtaining related training.

How to Use This Handbook

This handbook is divided into three major parts, each corresponding to one of the ''big picture'' chores project managers face when setting up and managing a project.

Part I: Your Deliverables, Phases, and Project Life Cycle

This part of the handbook will help you complete your first big chore: figuring out your **project life cycle**—in particular, figuring out how your project's major **deliverables (results)** will determine your appropriate **project phases** and how these phases may be grouped together to make up the ***life cycle*** of your project. This part presents a generic project life cycle, as well as a worksheet and suggestions that will help you develop your own customized project life cycle.

Part II: Your Essential Project Actions

This part of the handbook will help you complete your second big chore: figuring out which ***actions*** you need to take to complete your project. In other words, given the phases and life cycle you identified in Part I, what actions must you take to get the project done effectively? This section provides a list of project management best practices from which you may select those most applicable to your project.

Part III: Your Project Management Action Items

This part of the handbook will help you complete your third big chore: figuring out what specific steps to take to accomplish our essential project management actions. This is the heart of the handbook. It contains ***items*** in the form of worksheets, guidelines, and checklists to help guide you through each of the actions you identified as important in Part II. While you won't need to use every item for every project, you are likely to find that these items contain valuable solutions to many of your typical project problems.

Where to Begin

The table below will help you figure out where to begin.

If . . .	*Then . . .*
You are a new project manager working on your first project . . .	Work through Parts I and II; then refer to appropriate sections of Part III, as needed.
You are a first-time project manager working in an organization that has clearly prescribed for you your project's deliverables, phases, and project life cycles . . .	Skim through Part I and try to relate your organization's phases and life cycle to those presented in the text. Then work through Part II and appropriate sections of Part III.
You are an experienced project manager who is clear about your project's deliverables, phases, and appropriate life cycle . . .	Skip Part I. Skim through Part II and continue to appropriate sections of Part III.
You have a lot of experience managing projects, but would like to review some items and concepts . . .	Skim through the handbook, and challenge yourself by trying to apply any concepts or items to your company's procedures.

For an up-to-date list of references and other material relating to project management, visit my Web site at: www.michaelgreer.com.

PART I

YOUR DELIVERABLES, PHASES, AND PROJECT LIFE CYCLE

A *project* is a temporary endeavor undertaken to create a unique product or service.[1] Because projects by definition are temporary, project managers must make sure their projects are completed by expending only the amount of time, money, labor, and other resources that have been allocated. In addition, because projects result in unique products or services (deliverables), projects are typically organized into specific phases that most appropriately reflect the evolution of these unique deliverables. These project phases, taken as a whole, make up the overall life cycle of the project. Thus, the deliverables of your project, the project's phases, and your project's life cycle are inextricably linked. Let's look at each of these.

PROJECT DELIVERABLES

By *deliverables* we are referring to any measurable, tangible, verifiable output that must be produced to complete the project.[2] These may include *interim deliverables* (like scripts, system specifications, or blueprints) and *finished deliverables* (like the finished motion picture, software package, or completed building). Let's say you are creating a new product that will help your organization obtain a larger market share and greater profits. The deliverables for your project might include the following:

- An analysis of the market describing where your new product will fit in among its competitors and what specific needs it will meet in the marketplace
- A feasibility study detailing how your organization will be able to design, manufacture, and distribute the new product

- A description of the overall project concept
- A detailed project plan
- Product specifications (blueprints, flowcharts, etc.)
- A prototype or mock-up of the new product
- Tests of the new product using members of the product's target audience or buyers
- Enhancements or revisions to the new product based on the test results

Caution: It's easy to confuse deliverables and goals. Since *deliverables* are any measurable, tangible, verifiable items that must be produced to complete the project, they may be planned, observed, inspected, shaped, and, ultimately, described in contract specifications. *Goals,* on the other hand, while worth pursuing, are less tangible and therefore less easy to measure and track. For example, let's say that our goal is to build a sailboat that will be fast enough to win the America's Cup race. While this is a worthy goal, it is not the sort of thing that you could promise as a project deliverable. Instead, the project would more appropriately focus on deliverables such as building a boat with certain hull specifications, certain sail designs, and other specific and observable characteristics that we hope would help win the race. With luck, such a boat would enable our crew to beat the competition. However, whether we win or lose, the project would be judged a success if it produced a boat with the stated specifications within the schedule and budget allotted.

PROJECT PHASES

A *project phase* is a collection of project activities, usually resulting in the creation of a major deliverable.[3] Consider the list of deliverables above. There are literally hundreds of project activities that must be undertaken in order to complete all the deliverables listed. We could jump right in and try to complete all of these activities at once, but this would likely result in chaos. Instead, we combine the activities into clusters and sequence them so that we can proceed logically and systematically. In short, we group the project activities into phases. To continue our example, here are some appropriate project phases that would systematically yield the deliverables from our example above:

- *Phase I: Determine need and feasibility.* Complete all the detailed analysis work, including the market analysis, feasibility study, and overall project concept.
- *Phase II: Create the project plan.* After the need and feasibility are approved, complete all the activities necessary to create a detailed plan for completing the rest of the project.
- *Phase III: Create product specifications.* Create detailed product blueprints,

flowcharts, and so on. These would then be reviewed by outside experts and managers, then revised as needed.

- ***Phase IV: Create the prototype product.*** Complete all the activities necessary to create the prototype or mock-up.
- ***Phase V: Test and implement.*** Organize and conduct tests, make enhancements and revisions, and finalize the product.

Notice that the project phases are logically related to the deliverables we are creating. Within the phases, the deliverables evolve gradually, in successive approximations. In particular, the phases ensure that our new product provides plenty of opportunity for project players to review our results and make changes before too much time and money are spent.

A *milestone* is a significant event in the project, usually the completion of a major deliverable.[4] Typically, the completion of each project phase may be considered a milestone. For example, completion of the project plan is typically considered a milestone event. On a motion picture project, completion of the script is a milestone. Milestones differ from project to project depending on the type of deliverables the project is designed to create.

THE PROJECT LIFE CYCLE

The *project life cycle* is a collection of project phases whose name and number are determined by the control needs of the organization involved in the project.[5] For example, the five-phased sample project life cycle affords plenty of opportunity for control by the sponsoring organization. At the end of each phase, the project may be reviewed, deliverables may be revised, or the entire project may be stopped. In this way, the organization can protect its investment.

Because the types of deliverables resulting from projects differ widely from one industry to another, the project controls and phases used also can be quite different. For example, most film production projects include an editing or postproduction phase, while most homebuilding projects include a blueprint phase.

Different deliverables evolve in different ways, requiring different project phases. Yet no matter what the industry, *stakeholders*—those who are affected by project activities—review and approve deliverables at each phase before allowing the next phase to begin.[6] In this way, stakeholders try to assure that deliverables evolve in a steady, controlled fashion and that resources are not wasted.

Examples of typical project stakeholders include:

- The sponsor of the project (sometimes called the client, customer, owner, or funder)
- Suppliers, contractors, or vendors

- Professionals, craftspeople, and other specialists who serve on the project team
- The project manager
- Government agencies that regulate the project's processes or deliverables
- The public who will use or be affected by project outputs

Caution: It is important to identify and involve all project stakeholders so that everyone's expectations may be met. The last thing a project manager wants is to complete a project only to find out that a major stakeholder has been overlooked and is subsequently demanding that the project deliverables be changed.

As an industry matures, its typical project life cycles come to represent industry-wide "best practices." By using an industry-standard project life cycle, project managers can help ensure that deliverables will conform to recognized quality standards and that the project schedule and budget will be maintained. What's more, when you compare your project to the industry standard, you can quickly identify how your project will differ. This allows you to isolate activities that require especially thorough analysis and planning.

You may at some point find yourself in charge of planning and managing a project that doesn't seem to fit one of the industry-specific life cycles. In such situations, you can apply our Generic Project Life Cycle. It incorporates phases and activities that we believe are nearly universal in their application. The five phases of the Generic Project Life Cycle are illustrated in Figure 1.

Let's briefly examine each of these phases.

PHASE I: DETERMINE NEED AND FEASIBILITY

In this phase, the project manager and application specialists attempt to confirm that there is a need for the project deliverables. In addition, they try to decide whether the project is "doable"—that is, whether it is possible to plan and execute a project to create these deliverables.

ACTIVITIES

Activities that should be undertaken during this phase include, but are not limited to, the following:

- Goal definition
- Concept definition
- Needs analysis
- Market analysis
- Strategy definition
- Preliminary benefit-cost analysis[7]
- Preparation of project charter
- Review and approval of project charter

Figure 1. Project phases.

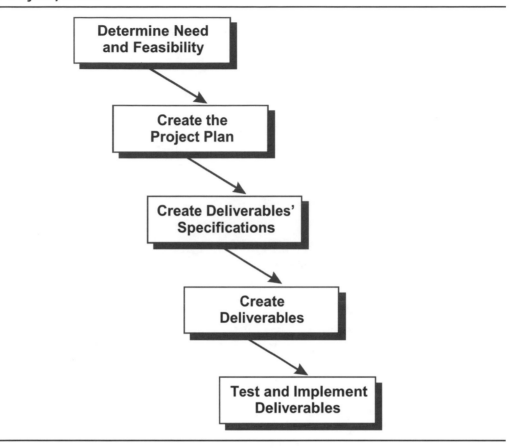

This phase culminates in a formal approval of the project concept or a go/no go decision.

PHASE II: CREATE THE PROJECT PLAN

Because projects are of finite duration and sometimes use unique work processes, the planning of a project is particularly important. In this phase, the project manager or application specialists create a formal document to guide the project team as they execute the project.

ACTIVITIES

Activities that should be undertaken during this phase include:

- Creating a formal planning document that may be used to:
  —Link project activities to expressed needs and feasibility studies (i.e., tying the plan to the outputs of Phase I: Determine Need and Feasibility).

—Provide a written record of assumptions regarding deliverables, work processes, resources required, and so forth.

—Document the detailed analysis of project requirements by creating network diagrams, work breakdown structure (WBS), schedule, budget, and other planning artifacts.

—Help communicate clearly among stakeholders.

—Provide a written record of agreed-on scope, costs, and schedule.

—Facilitate a critique of project assumptions by stakeholders.

- Getting the project plan approved by sponsors and other stakeholders before project work begins.[8]

PHASE III: CREATE DELIVERABLES' SPECIFICATIONS

In this phase, application specialists create a formal document that describes in substantial detail the deliverables to be created—for example:

- Software design documents
- Blueprints for a building
- A detailed media treatment for a videotape production

It's important to distinguish the extensive Phase III deliverables' specifications from the preliminary specifications created as part of the Phase II planning process. In the Phase II planning process, the project team describes the deliverables in just enough detail to create a project plan. Once the plan is approved, the project team may begin spending resources (including time and money) on the project. Thus, it is simply good business to wait until Phase III to extend the preliminary specifications. At this time they should be fleshed out substantially so that project stakeholders can evaluate them at length. In this way, the project team can make modifications on paper instead of reworking the deliverables.

Note: These detailed specifications sometimes identify unanticipated deliverables. Therefore, this phase often includes descriptions of ways in which schedules or budgets need to be refined, as well as new project assumptions.

ACTIVITIES

Activities that should be undertaken during this phase include:

- Creating one or more documents describing deliverables' specifications in substantial detail
- Obtaining approval of the deliverables' specifications from sponsors and other stakeholders[9]

PHASE IV: CREATE DELIVERABLES

The most time-consuming and resource-intense phase of the project is the phase in which the project deliverables are created according to the approved deliverable specifications. In other words, to extend our Phase III examples, the software is developed, the building is built, the videotape is produced, and so on.

The specific activities involved in this phase differ dramatically from one industry or application to another. For example, a defense contractor may first need to create a working model to prove the concept works before building the full-blown version of the defense system. Or a software developer will likely create and test small units of code before programming and integrating all software modules. And a video producer would likely create scripts, conduct casting sessions and rehearsals, and produce other interim deliverables prior to engaging in full-blown production activities.

ACTIVITIES

Activities that should be undertaken during this phase include, but are by no means limited to, the following:

- Creating prototypes of deliverables
- Creating portions or pieces of deliverables
- Providing services as promised in the project plan
- Completing fully integrated deliverables
- Obtaining sponsor and other stakeholder approval of each deliverable or service provided, as appropriate[10]

PHASE V: TEST AND IMPLEMENT DELIVERABLES

In this phase, the project deliverables are shown to work as planned and are turned over to the sponsor or customer for use. As in Phase IV, the specific activities involved in this phase differ dramatically from one industry or application to another. The defense contractor will likely test and refine the product and manufacturing processes many times prior to full production and deployment. The software producer is likely to run user tests and make revisions prior to delivery to the customer. And the video producer may conduct audience tests of rough cuts prior to final editing and delivery to the client.

ACTIVITIES

Activities that should be undertaken during this phase include, but are certainly not limited to, the following:

- Testing of deliverables, together or in parts
- Refinement of deliverables based on test results
- Implementation of deliverables on a limited basis (such as a field trial)
- Further refinement of deliverables based on preliminary implementation
- Full production of final deliverables
- Sponsor or other stakeholder approval of test results, resulting plans for modification of deliverables, and final deliverables[11]

ASSIGNMENT: YOUR UNIQUE PROJECT LIFE CYCLE

Bearing in mind your project's unique deliverables, use the My Unique Project Life Cycle worksheet to determine your project's unique phases and life cycles.

WORKSHEET: My Unique Project Life Cycle

Instructions: This item will help you to create your own custom-tailored project life cycle—one that best reflects the unique requirements of your project's deliverables and your organization. Using the first two columns as examples, fill in the third column with between three and seven broad phases that your project should employ. In the last column, note the key activities that will be essential to the success of each phase. (Continue on the back of the page, if necessary.)

Typical Project Phases	*Typical Project Activities*	*My Project's Phases*	*My Project's Activities*
Determine Need and Feasibility *Purpose:* Confirm that project is needed, do-able; formal go/no go approval.	- Goal and concept definition - Needs or market analysis - Strategy definition - Preliminary benefit-cost analysis		
Create the Project Plan *Purpose:* Create a formal document to guide the project team as they execute the project.	- Involve stakeholders in specifying and agreeing on project outcomes and methodology - Create written record of assumptions, agreed-on scope, resources, schedule, costs, etc. - Obtain consensus and formal approval		

Typical Project Phases	Typical Project Activities	My Project's Phases	My Project's Activities
Create Deliverables' Specifications ***Purpose:*** Describe the deliverables in substantial detail on paper.	■ Create design plans, flowcharts, blueprints, media treatments, and other "on-paper" deliverables' descriptions and samples as appropriate ■ Circulate and obtain feedback, revise, and obtain formal approval		
Create Deliverables ***Purpose:*** Create prototypes, pieces; create full-blown, fully integrated deliverables	■ Create all promised deliverables, in chunks or complete ■ Provide planned services, execute planned activities, obtain formal approval		
Test and Implement Deliverables ***Purpose:*** Make sure project deliverables work as planned; turn over to sponsor for use	■ Testing of deliverables (in whole or in part) ■ Refinement, revision ■ Full production, implementation, and final approval		

PART II

YOUR ESSENTIAL PROJECT ACTIONS

Given the deliverables and phases you identified in Part I, what actions must you take to get the project done effectively? This part provides a review of essential PM (project management) *processes* as identified in the Project Management Institute's *PMBOK (Project Management Body of Knowledge)*.[1] In addition, we provide a list of essential PM actions derived from those processes from which you may select those most applicable to your project.

PROJECT MANAGEMENT PROCESSES

In Part I we identified three important *whats* related to the project:

- What are the deliverables to be created?
- What are the phases by which we will organize the project?
- What is our overall project life cycle?

Now it's time to consider some of the *hows* related to the project:

- How will we move from phase to phase within the project?
- How should the project manager determine specific assignments and "to-dos" for the project team?
- In short, how will we take action to complete the project?

The answers to these questions may be found by examining the essential project management processes. A *process* may be defined as a series of actions designed to bring about specific results.[2] There are five processes that should be applied to each phase of a project in order to bring about the completion of the phase:

1. Initiating
2. Planning

3. Executing
4. Controlling
5. Closing

Three of these processes (planning, executing, and controlling) apply to any type of management activity, whether it involves a project or an ongoing operation.[3] Since projects are temporary (i.e., they have an identifiable starting point and require timely completion), they must also include the processes of initiating (starting up) and closing (formally accepting the results and ending the phase).[4]

Note that all of these processes eventually become unconscious habits of effective project managers. Through practicing them in a conscious way at first, you can eventually internalize them and begin to move among them in a fluid way, helping to ensure your project's success. Figure 2 illustrates how these project management processes are linked. Let's take a closer look at each of these processes.

INITIATING

Initiating means getting a project or project phase authorized. It involves obtaining the organization's commitment to the project as a whole. Alternately, initiating may involve getting the organization's commitment that a particular project phase should be started.[5]

Typically, the sponsor, customer, or person providing the funds gives the authorization to begin a project or phase. So, in effect, initiating means getting the green light from the client to begin work on the project as a whole or on one phase.

PLANNING

Planning is of major importance on a project because by definition the project involves creating something unique.[6] In other words, you may be heading into un-

Figure 2. Project management processes.

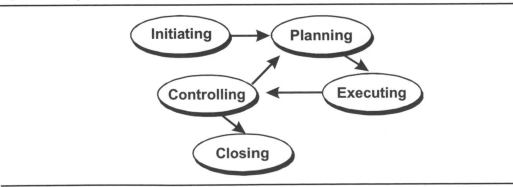

Source: Project Management Institute, *A Guide to the Project Management Body of Knowledge* (Upper Darby, PA: Project Management Institute, 1994).

charted waters, so you should have a plan to help you get through them safely. There are two types of planning: essential planning and discretionary planning.

ESSENTIAL PLANNING

Essential planning consists of four subprocesses:

- Defining the scope (all the products and services to be provided by the project)
- Identifying or defining the required activities, resources, and schedule
- Creating detailed cost estimates and budgets
- Integrating all of the above into a comprehensive project plan

We call these subprocesses essential because no one should undertake a project or project phase without first completing all four of them.[7]

DISCRETIONARY PLANNING

Discretionary planning processes are desirable but not necessarily required to complete a project.[8] These processes are performed as needed and include creation of formal plans such as these:

- Quality plan
- Communications plan
- Staffing plan (over and above that described in the essential plan)
- Procurement plan
- Risk assessment and response plan
- Other formal plans dictated by organizational values and policies

Some veteran project managers would no doubt argue that adopting one or more of these plans is not simply discretionary but essential. Depending on your organization and your industry, you may agree. At a minimum, you should quickly skim through the Action Item in Part III associated with each of these planning processes and decide whether it might apply to your project; if it clearly does not apply, then you can reject it. In this way, you will be sure that you have done your job as project manager by challenging all assumptions about the work process, selecting the best possible approaches, and taking nothing for granted.

In any case, whether you classify the particular outputs as essential or discretionary, planning is a vital process of project management. As you will see in Part III, the majority of the Action Items in this handbook are designed to support the planning process.

EXECUTING

Executing is the process by which project plans are carried out. Executing involves several subprocesses:

- **Project Plan Execution**—carrying out the project plan as written (e.g., building the house, producing the motion picture, developing the new software, or carrying out whatever activities the plan called for)[9]
- **Team Development**—developing individual and group skills to enhance project performance (e.g., formal and informal training, coaching)
- **Information Distribution**—making needed information available to project stakeholders in a timely manner
- **Solicitation**—obtaining quotations, bids, offers, or proposals from contractors, vendors, or other providers of essential goods or services
- **Source Selection**—choosing from among potential contractors, vendors, or providers
- **Contract Administration**—managing the relationship with the contractor, vendor, or other provider, including such activities as handling paperwork and ensuring payment

CONTROLLING

Controlling involves comparing actual performance with planned performance. In other words, are you doing exactly what you planned to do? If you discover deviations from the plan (often called *variances*), you must analyze these variances and figure out alternative actions that will get the project back on track. You can then decide which alternative is best and take appropriate corrective action.[10] Controlling involves several subprocesses:

- **Progress Reporting**—collecting and disseminating progress information to all project stakeholders
- **Overall Change Control**—coordinating changes across the entire project
- **Scope Change Control**—controlling changes to project scope, which often means limiting the project's deliverables to only those planned
- **Cost Control**—controlling changes to the project budget
- **Quality Control**—monitoring specific project results to determine if they comply with relevant quality standards and identifying ways to eliminate causes of unsatisfactory performance
- **Quality Assurance**—evaluating overall project performance regularly to provide confidence that the project will satisfy the relevant quality standards
- **Risk Control**—attempting to minimize the effect that unknowns or potentially negative events will have on the project[11]

CLOSING

Because projects are temporary endeavors, projects and project phases must eventually come to an end. But who is to say when a project or phase has ended? More important, how do you know when to stop expending effort and money on a project or project phase?

Projects typically involve many stakeholders, each of whom is likely to have an opinion about the suitability of deliverables. To help prevent disputes, it is necessary to set up a formal process by which the project or project phase may be declared officially completed. This formal process is called *closing*. Closing involves formally accepting the results and ending the project or phase. This includes several subprocesses:

- **Scope Verification**—ensuring that all identified project deliverables have been completely satisfied
- **Administrative Closure**—generating, gathering, and disseminating information to formalize project completion, often including sign-off or written approval of the deliverables or phase
- **Contract Close-Out**—completion and settlement of the contract, including resolution of any outstanding items[12]

Note: Clear-cut and effective closing is based on the formal project plan. The project plan should spell out exactly what the deliverables will look like, how and by whom the deliverables will be approved, and so on. By formally agreeing to the plan, the stakeholders have in advance agreed to specific deliverables to be created by specific methods. In this way, the finished results can be compared to the planned results, thus minimizing disputes over whether the deliverables are suitable.

PROJECT PHASES AND THE PROJECT MANAGEMENT PROCESSES

The life cycle of a project and the processes used to manage the project are distinct and separate yet inextricably linked. The project manager uses the processes in order to complete each phase of the life cycle. Figure 3 illustrates how the phases and processes interrelate.

Note that the project life cycle is essentially linear: each phase results in a work product that is passed on to the next phase. The project deliverables evolve gradually, culminating in the finished product. On the other hand, the project management processes are nonlinear. They recur over and over again throughout the project, in all phases.

The project life cycle influences the final deliverables by identifying the essential outputs of each phase. In contrast, the project management processes influence the

Figure 3. Project phases and the project management processes.

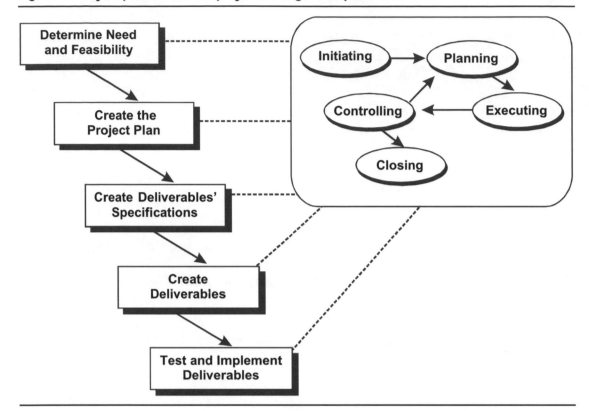

project manager by identifying the actions that he or she must take to help make the project a success.

ASSIGNMENT: YOUR ESSENTIAL PROJECT ACTIONS

Bearing in mind your project's unique deliverables, phases, and life cycle, use the Summary of Key Project Manager Actions and Results worksheet to determine the essential actions you must take as project manager to complete your project.

WORKSHEET: Summary of Key Project Manager Actions and Results

Instructions: This worksheet contains a list of actions that project managers should take in order to complete a project successfully. Beside each action is a description of one or more specific results that the action should produce. Place a check mark beside each action and result that will be essential to your project's success.

INITIATING	
Action	*Results of Successful Performance*
1. Demonstrate Project Need and Feasibility	■ A document confirming that there is a need for the project deliverables and describing in broad terms: the deliverables, means of creating the deliverables, costs of creating and implementing the deliverables, benefits to be obtained by implementing the deliverables
2. Obtain Project Authorization	■ A go/no go decision is made by the sponsor ■ A project manager is assigned ■ A project charter is created that: —Formally recognizes the project —Is issued by a manager external to the project and at a high enough organizational level to meet project needs —Authorizes the project manager to apply resources to the project activities
3. Obtain Authorization for the Phase	■ A go/no go decision is made by the sponsor that authorizes the project manager to apply organizational resources to the activities of a particular phase ■ Written approval of the phase is created that: —Formally recognizes the existence of the phase —Is issued by a manager external to the project and at a high enough organizational level to meet the project needs
PLANNING	
4. Describe Project Scope	■ Statement of project scope ■ Scope management plan ■ Work breakdown structure
5. Define and Sequence Project Activities	■ An activity list (a list of all activities that will be performed on the project) ■ Updates to the work breakdown structure (WBS) ■ A project network diagram
6. Estimate Duration for Activities and Resources Required	■ Estimate of duration (time required) for each activity and assumptions related to each estimate ■ Statement of resource requirements ■ Updates to the activity list
7. Develop a Project Schedule	■ Project schedule in the form of Gantt charts, network diagrams, milestone charts, or text tables ■ Supporting details, such as resource usage over time, cash flow projections, and order and delivery schedules
8. Estimate Costs	■ Cost estimates for completing each activity ■ Supporting detail, including assumptions and constraints ■ Cost management plan describing how cost variances will be handled

(continues)

9. Build a Budget and Spending Plan	▪ A cost baseline or time-phased budget for measuring and monitoring costs ▪ A spending plan, telling how much will be spent on what resources at what time
10. **(Optional):** Create a Formal Quality Plan	▪ A quality management plan, including operational definitions ▪ Quality verification checklists
11. **(Optional):** Create a Formal Project Communications Plan	▪ A communication management plan, including: —Collection structure —Distribution structure —Description of information to be disseminated —Schedules listing when information will be produced —A method for updating the communications plan
12. Organize and Acquire Staff	▪ Role and responsibility assignments ▪ Staffing plan ▪ Organizational chart with detail, as appropriate ▪ Project staff ▪ Project team directory
13. **(Optional):** Identify Risks and Plan to Respond	▪ A document describing potential risks, including their sources, symptoms, and ways to address them
14. **(Optional):** Plan for and Acquire Outside Resources	▪ Procurement management plan describing how contractors will be obtained ▪ Statement of work (SOW) or statement of requirements (SOR) describing the item (product or service) to be procured ▪ Bid documents, such as RFP (request for proposal), IFB (invitation for bid) ▪ Evaluation criteria—means of scoring contractors' proposals ▪ Contract with one or more suppliers of goods or services
15. Organize the Project Plan	▪ A comprehensive project plan that pulls together all the outputs of the preceding project planning activities
16. Close Out the Project Planning Phase	▪ A project plan that has been approved, in writing, by the sponsor ▪ A green light, or okay, to begin work on the project
17. Revisit the Project Plan and Replan, If Needed	▪ Confidence that the detailed plans to execute a particular phase are still accurate and will effectively achieve results as planned
EXECUTING	
18. Execute Project Activities	▪ Work results (deliverables) are created ▪ Change requests (i.e., based on expanded or contracted project) are identified

	■ Periodic progress reports are created ■ Team performance is assessed, guided, and improved, if needed ■ Bids and proposals for deliverables are solicited, contractors (suppliers) are chosen, and contracts are established ■ Contracts are administered to achieve desired work results
CONTROLLING	
19. Control Project Activities	■ Decision to accept inspected deliverables ■ Corrective actions such as rework of deliverables and adjustments to work process ■ Updates to project plan and scope ■ List of lessons learned ■ Improved quality ■ Completed evaluation checklists (if applicable)
CLOSING	
20. Close Out Project Activities	■ Formal acceptance, documented in writing, that the sponsor has accepted the product of this phase or activity ■ Formal acceptance of contractor work products and updates to the contractor's files ■ Updated project records prepared for archiving ■ A plan for follow-up and/or hand-off of work products

PHASES, PROCESSES, AND ACTION ITEMS: PULLING IT ALL TOGETHER

I have described five generic project phases that may be used as a baseline to organize nearly any project and five processes that project managers need to perform in order to complete these project phases.

But how do these elements fit together? The following table makes the connections clear. Here's how to use it:

1. Figure out which phase your project is in (refer to the left column).
2. Decide which project management processes you need to complete (refer to the middle column).
3. Identify the relevant Action Items that can help you perform the process (refer to the right column).
4. Turn to Part III and locate the relevant Action Items.
5. Skim through them and decide how you can put them to work for you. Make additions or deletions as appropriate to accommodate your particular industry or organization.

IF . . . *You are in this generic* *project phase*	*. . . AND* *You want to perform* *this process*	*. . . THEN* *Refer to these* *Action Items*
Phase I: Determine Need and Feasibility *(Define goals, concept; analyze need, market; define strategy; do benefit-cost analysis)*	Initiating Phase I Planning Phase I Executing Phase I Controlling Phase I	■ Demonstrate Project Need and Feasibility
	Closing Phase I	■ Obtain Project Authorization
Phase II: Create the Project Plan *(Make a record of all planned deliverables, work processes, resources, scope, and so on, and get it approved)*	Initiating Phase II	■ Obtain Authorization for the Phase
	Planning Phase II Executing Phase II Controlling Phase II	■ Describe Project Scope ■ Define and Sequence Project Activities ■ Estimate Duration for Activities and Resources Required ■ Develop a Project Schedule ■ Estimate Costs ■ Build a Budget and Spending Plan ■ **(Optional)**: Create a Formal Quality Plan ■ **(Optional)**: Create a Formal Project Communications Plan ■ Organize and Acquire Staff ■ **(Optional)**: Plan for and Acquire Outside Resources ■ Organize the Project Plan
	Closing Phase II	■ Close Out the Project Planning Phase
Phase III: Create Deliverables Specifications *(Describe deliverables in detail; get description approved)*	Initiating Phase III	■ Obtain Authorization for the Phase
	Planning Phase III Executing Phase III Controlling Phase III	■ Revisit the Project Plan and Replan, if Needed ■ Execute Project Activities ■ Control Project Activitie
	Closing Phase III	■ Close Out Project Activities
Phase IV: Create Deliverables *(Create prototype pieces; full-blown, fully integrated deliverables; get them approved)*	Initiating Phase IV	■ Obtain Authorization for the Phase
	Planning Phase IV	■ Revisit the Project Plan and Replan, if Needed
	Executing Phase IV Controlling Phase IV	■ Execute Project Activities ■ Control Project Activities
	Closing Phase IV	■ Close Out Project Activities
Phase V: Test and Implement Deliverables *(Test, refine, produce, and install deliverables)*	Initiating Phase V	■ Obtain Authorization for the Phase
	Planning Phase V	■ Revisit the Project Plan and Replan, if Needed
	Executing Phase V Controlling Phase V	■ Execute Project Activities ■ Control Project Activities
	Closing Phase V	■ Close Out Project Activities

PART III

YOUR PROJECT MANAGEMENT ACTION ITEMS

OVERVIEW

This section provides specific items to help you work through each of the five project management processes:

- Initiating
- Planning
- Executing
- Controlling
- Closing

For detailed explanations of these processes, see Part II.
Each Action Item in this part is divided into sections:

- *Assignment*—a description of the assignment or specific project management task that this Action Item will support
- *Desired Outputs*—the results that should be achieved when you complete this Action Item
- *Background Information*—just enough background to help you better understand the Action Item
- *Worksheet and/or Guidelines*—a set of step-by-step procedures to guide you through the completion of the Action Item
- *What a Veteran Project Manager Might Do*—more sophisticated strategies or specific practices that seasoned project management professionals might use to complete the Action Item. Most of the processes described here require further training or support before the new manager can implement them.

- *Pitfalls and Cautions*—some common mistakes made by novices and suggestions for avoiding these mistakes
- *For More Information*—references you might want to examine for further details

All of the Action Items are listed next, organized according to the project management process they support.

Initiating

- Action Item: Demonstrate Project Need and Feasibility
- Action Item: Obtain Project Authorization
- Action Item: Obtain Authorization for the Phase

Planning

- Action Item: Describe Project Scope
- Action Item: Define and Sequence Project Activities
- Action Item: Estimate Durations for Activities and Resources Required
- Action Item: Develop a Project Schedule
- Action Item: Estimate Costs
- Action Item: Build a Budget and Spending Plan
- Optional Action Item: Create a Formal Quality Plan
- Optional Action Item: Create a Formal Project Communications Plan
- Action Item: Organize and Acquire Staff
- Optional Action Item: Identify Risks and Plan to Respond
- Optional Action Item: Plan for and Acquire Outside Resources
- Action Item: Organize the Project Plan
- Action Item: Close Out the Project Planning Phase
- Action Item: Revisit the Project Plan and Replan If Needed

Executing

- Action Item: Execute Project Activities

Controlling

- Action Item: Control Project Activities

Closing

- Action Item: Close Out Project Activities

Remember: In the discussion of Action Items, the term *sponsor* means customer, client, final owner of the project, or entity providing funding—in short, the person who has the power to provide funds, approve the use of resources, and stop the project.

INITIATING

Initiating means getting the project authorized. It involves obtaining the organization's commitment to the project as a whole. Alternately, initiating may involve getting the organization's commitment that a particular project phase will be started.[1]

The following Action Items support the process of initiating:

- Action Item: Demonstrate Project Need and Feasibility
- Action Item: Obtain Project Authorization
- Action Item: Obtain Authorization for the Phase

ACTION ITEM: DEMONSTRATE PROJECT NEED AND FEASIBILITY

ASSIGNMENT

Decide whether you have enough information to prove to the sponsor that the project is needed and feasible.

DESIRED OUTPUTS

- A document confirming that there is a need for the project deliverables; this would describe the following items in broad terms:
  —The project goal and/or underlying concepts
  —The deliverables
  —By what means the deliverables might be created
  —The costs of creating and implementing the deliverables
  —The benefits to be obtained by implementing the deliverables
  —Who are the sponsors and stakeholders
  —In what ways the sponsors and stakeholders are prepared to support the project

BACKGROUND INFORMATION

The purpose of Phase I: Determine Need and Feasibility is to obtain authorization for the project. Authorization means formal approval from the sponsor. Circumstances under which authorization can usually be obtained include the presence of a legitimate:[2]

- Market demand
- Business need
- Customer request
- Technological advance
- Legal requirement

In recent years, many enterprises have established a project office to serve as a clearinghouse for projects. Made up of high-level managers from all of the enterprise's functional units, the project office typically evaluates individual project proposals in the light of the enterprise's long-term strategic goals and the overall project load of the entire enterprise and all of its resources. In this way, overbooking of resources and duplication of effort by different project teams working toward similar goals can be avoided. (In addition, a typical project office provides some administrative support for project management, such as specialized PM software and the people to run it, as well as organization-specific PM items and processes, PM coaching, and formal training.)

If your organization has such a project office, you and your sponsor should obtain information about the ways in which projects are selected for approval. In particular, you should obtain a list of any criteria used to prioritize or to reject project proposals prior to their authorization.

Before you can obtain authorization for your project, you will need to demonstrate to the sponsoring organization that you have done adequate research and that the project is needed and doable.

WORKSHEET: Demonstrating Project Need and Feasibility

Instructions: This worksheet is designed to help you decide whether you've done your homework and obtained enough information to prove to your sponsor that the project you propose is needed and feasible.

Evaluate your project documentation to date by asking yourself each of these questions. (Alternately, you might have a colleague or project supporter review the document with the sponsor's point of view in mind.) Check "Yes" for the ones you have answered adequately. If you check "No," review the italicized follow-up suggestion and figure out what to do next.

Yes	No	Questions
		Have I defined the project goal and core concept clearly, in terms the sponsor* can understand? *If no, redefine the goal statement and have it checked by someone who thinks like the sponsor.*
		Is the sponsor financially and organizationally able to provide all needed support? *If no, who is the real sponsor, and how can we get the real sponsor involved?*
		Does a market analysis or needs analysis show a bona fide need for the product (deliverables) of the project? *If no, consider abandoning the project or conducting an appropriate analysis that proves project need.*
		Have we clearly expressed the costs and benefits of the project? *If no, restate the description of costs and benefits and have it checked by someone who thinks like the sponsor.*

Yes	No	*Questions*
		Have I consulted all project stakeholders to obtain their opinions about the need and feasibility? *If no, identify missing stakeholders and review the need and feasibility with them, asking for feedback.*
		Have we defined a project strategy in enough detail to enable the sponsors to really understand what they're getting into? *If no, restate the project strategy and have it checked by someone who thinks like the sponsor.*
		Have I assembled the results of my research into a well-written document or presentation? *If no, create your document or presentation, and have it checked by someone who thinks like the sponsor.*
		Have I determined an appropriate audience and scheduled a time, place, and date for presenting my project proposal? *If no, discuss these items with your supervisor (or a more experienced project manager), and figure out what to do next.*
		Have I rehearsed the presentation, including my answers to potentially controversial questions? *If no, plan and conduct such a rehearsal.*

Sponsor is the customer, client, final owner, or entity providing funding. The sponsor has the power to provide funds, approve the use of resources, and/or stop the project.

WHAT A VETERAN PROJECT MANAGER MIGHT DO

A project management professional might take these forms of action:

- Assess the organization's political landscape and figure out how the project might support or conflict with the explicit or hidden agendas that people in the organization are pursuing.
- Gradually build consensus regarding project need and feasibility by actively networking among key recommenders or decision makers.
- Pitch (sell) the proposal or presentation according to the needs and "hot buttons" of individual stakeholders or sponsors.
- Use various decision models, such as decision trees or the analytical hierarchy process, to compare project approaches and score the benefits contributed by different approaches.[3]
- Use constrained optimization methods (mathematical models or multiobjective programming algorithms) to decide among project alternatives.[4]
- Assemble a team of subject-matter experts to help refine the statement of need or feasibility.[5] This can help challenge erroneous planning assumptions, avoid pitfalls, and enhance the plans by refining them so that they include a

greater level of detail. What's more, subject-matter experts often volunteer opinions outside our areas of expertise, thus encouraging us to "think outside the box."

PITFALLS AND CAUTIONS

Most successful projects draw their energy from a core team of people who are deeply committed to the project's goals from its inception. These people may be an informal group made up of like-minded colleagues or a formally appointed task force. Whatever their relationship, they typically work together to brainstorm project definition and form alliances to promote the project to sponsors and stakeholders.

Unfortunately, some novice project managers, possibly wishing to appear strong or self-reliant, have been known to overlook the value of such a core team, preferring instead to work alone on behalf of the project. This is counterproductive. Without a strong base of organizational support, most projects are simply undoable. I recommend that novice project managers take the time to assemble (formally or informally) a group of people who support the project's goals and can help define and promote it. Particularly in the early stages, project managers need all the help (and co-counseling!) they can get.

Another pitfall for the novice manager is assuming that the project's need and feasibility are self-evident and shared by everyone who is discussing the project. Unfortunately, it is often the case that the sponsor and key stakeholders each have significantly different pictures of the project need and how project results will be achieved. These differing pictures can lead to all sorts of different assumptions about work process, costs, time frames, and so on. Therefore, it's essential to bring these pictures into alignment before beginning the project and expending the organization's resources. It's the project manager's job to provide sponsors and key stakeholders with as much detail about the project as possible and to forge a consensus regarding its need and feasibility. One important way to do this is to *get people's ideas in writing!* Document in detail everyone's assumptions about the project's need and feasibility so everyone can be "singing from the same songbook."

FOR MORE INFORMATION . . .

See PMI's *PMBOK* item 5.1, Initiation.

Block, Thomas R., and Frame, J. Davidson. *The Project Office.* Menlo Park, CA: Crisp Publications, 1998.

Graham, Robert J., and Englund, Randall L. *Creating an Environment for Successful Projects: The Quest to Manage Project Management.* San Francisco: Jossey-Bass, 1997.

ACTION ITEM: OBTAIN PROJECT AUTHORIZATION

ASSIGNMENT

Obtain suitable authorization from the sponsor to begin the project.

DESIRED OUTPUTS

- A go/no go decision is made by the sponsor.
  —If no go, all planning typically stops.
  —If go, the next items apply.
- A project manager is identified and assigned.[6]
- A project charter is created that:[7]
  —Formally recognizes the existence of the project.
  —Is supported by a manager external to the project and at a high enough organizational level so that he or she can support project needs.
  —Authorizes the project manager to apply organizational resources (people, equipment, materials) to project activities.

BACKGROUND INFORMATION

Authorization means *formal approval* from the sponsor. Formal approval should:

- Identify a specific project manager to continue project planning activities into the next phase.
- Consist of a written project charter outlining the items listed above.

Remember: The project manager's responsibilities should be matched by an equal amount of authority to execute those responsibilities. This authority must be expressed as clearly and as formally as the responsibilities.

WORKSHEET: Is This Project Authorized?

Instructions: This worksheet will help you figure out whether you have been fully authorized to continue with the project you proposed. Assuming that you have been given some form of approval to begin the project, evaluate that approval to determine if it provides you with the authority you need in order to do the job. If you check "No," review the italicized follow-up suggestion and figure out what to do next. **Remember:** *If the project isn't authorized, you probably should not be expending resources (including your own time) working on it.*

If you are working with a formal or informal advisory group, you might ask its members to complete this worksheet with you.

Yes	No	Criteria
		Has the project been formally recognized as a project by one or more sponsors? *If no, find out why not, and discuss with your supervisor or the potential sponsor what to do next.*
		Has news of the project been widely circulated in written form? *If no, find out why not, and figure out what to do next.*
		Has project authorization been issued by a manager external to the project and at a high enough organizational level to help meet project needs? *If no, identify an appropriate sponsoring manager, and figure out how you can get his or her authorization.*
		Has the project manager been clearly identified? *If no, find out who should identify the project manager and what steps are needed to get the project manager officially identified.*
		Is the project manager authorized to apply organizational resources (people, equipment, materials) to project activities? *If the project manager has not been formally authorized, then ask the sponsor by whose authority project resources will be applied.*
		Has the project manager been given the green light to move on to the next project phase, preferably through formal sign-off* by the project sponsor? *If no, decide what conditions need to be met to get authorization, and begin to meet them.*

*See Action Item: Close Out Project Activities for a sample sign-off form.

WORKSHEET: The Project Charter

Project Name: _____ **Date:** _____

Project Manager: _____

Project Tracking Number: _____

Project Justification (problem or opportunity addressed):

Overview of Deliverables (high-level, broad-brush only; provide details, if any, in appendixes—for example, needs analysis/feasibility study notes, detailed work breakdown structure, preliminary schedule, preliminary cost estimate, sample deliverables, background memos and reports, organization chart of project team, others as needed):

Specific Project Objectives and Success Criteria (schedule, cost, quality):

Primary Stakeholders and Roles (including broad statement of roles and responsibilities of all customers, sponsors, contributors, reviewers, managers, sign-off authorities, project manager, etc.):

Key Assumptions (including broad statement of sponsor and stakeholder inputs and resources to be provided, as well as a delineation of what's outside project scope):

Signatures of those who agree that the above information is accurate:

- Project team members:

- Project sponsor and/or authorizing manager(s):

WHAT A VETERAN PROJECT MANAGER MIGHT DO

No matter what the project size or complexity, the project manager should obtain adequate, formal authorization and support. A seasoned project manager might undertake some of these activities to obtain support for the project:

- Assess the organization's political situation and figure out how the project might support or conflict with the explicit or hidden agendas that people in the organization are pursuing.
- Gradually build consensus regarding the project by actively networking among key recommenders or decision makers.
- Pitch (sell) the project according to the needs and hot buttons of individual stakeholders or sponsors.

A seasoned project manager might undertake some of these activities to clarify his or her authority:

- Create a thorough project charter with the details of authorization clearly spelled out. Draw on past project charters for boilerplate text and ideas.
- Present the charter to the sponsor and ask for formal approval by a written sign-off—in effect, making a contract between the sponsor and the project manager.

PITFALLS AND CAUTIONS

A new project manager eager to get the project started and show initiative might want to begin work with nothing more than a handshake or verbal approval. This is risky, since the project manager is assuming the authority to expend the organization's valuable resources. Ask yourself: "If I begin work without written authorization, who will back me up if we run into trouble?"

Always get written approval to begin the project, and make sure you have adequate authority to make job assignments, spend money, use equipment, and so on. Otherwise, you may find yourself all alone out on a limb when problems occur.

FOR MORE INFORMATION . . .

See PMI's *PMBOK* item 5.1, Initiation.

ACTION ITEM: OBTAIN AUTHORIZATION FOR THE PHASE

Note: Whether you will need authorization to begin each phase will depend on the type of project and the organizations involved. Initial approval of the entire project may be enough to initiate authorization of each project phase automatically. However, see the Pitfalls and Cautions section.

ASSIGNMENT

Obtain suitable authorization from the sponsor to begin a particular project phase.

DESIRED OUTPUTS

- A go/no go decision is made by the sponsor, concerning whether the project manager will be authorized to apply organizational resources (people, equipment, materials) to the activities of a particular phase (as opposed to the entire project).
  —If no go, all work typically stops.
  —If go, continue with the next items.
- The phase is given written approval that:[8]
  —Formally recognizes the existence of the phase.
  —Is supported by a manager external to the project and at a high enough organizational level so that he or she can support the needs of the phase.
  —Authorizes the project manager to apply organizational resources (people, equipment, materials) to the activities of the phase.

BACKGROUND INFORMATION

Each project phase produces deliverables that can be examined and approved. In fact, one of the main benefits of dividing a project into phases is that it allows stakeholders to evaluate project deliverables as they are evolving, before it's too late (or too costly) to make modifications. This can prevent the team from creating deliverables that are far afield of the stakeholders' vision. Stakeholder review, input, and authorization of each phase are essential.

Authorization means *formal approval* from the sponsor. Formal approval should consist of a brief, formally written statement (with copies to appropriate stakeholders) indicating that the results of the previous phase are acceptable and that the project manager may proceed to the next phase.

Remember: The project manager's responsibilities should be matched by an equal amount of authority to execute those responsibilities. This authority must be expressed as clearly and as formally as the responsibilities.

WORKSHEET: Is This Phase Really Authorized?

Instructions: This worksheet will help you figure out whether you have been fully authorized to begin a project phase. Assuming that you have been given some form of approval to begin the phase, evaluate that approval to determine if it provides you with the authority you need to do the job. If you check "No," review the italicized follow-up suggestion and figure out what to do next.

   If you are working with a formal or informal advisory group, you might ask its members to complete this worksheet with you.

   Remember: If the phase isn't authorized, you probably should not be expending resources (including your own time) working on it!

Yes	No	Criteria
		Is the phase we are about to begin part of a project that has been formally recognized as a project? *If no, return to Action Item: Obtain Project Authorization.*
		Have all appropriate stakeholders approved the results of the preceding phase? *If no, consider how and why the results of the preceding phase were not approved. Ask yourself: "Should we really continue to the next phase without reworking the deliverables, changing the formal project specifications, or otherwise changing our project plans?"*
		Has the authorization for this phase been issued by a manager external to the project and at a high enough organizational level to help meet project needs? *If no, identify an appropriate sponsoring manager, and figure out how you can get his or her authorization.*
		Is it clear who the project manager is for this phase? *If no, find out who should identify the project manager and what steps are needed to get the manager officially identified.*
		Is the project manager authorized to apply organizational resources (people, equipment, materials) to the phase? *If the project manager has not been formally authorized, then ask the sponsor by whose authority project resources will be applied.*
		Has the project manager been given the green light to continue with this project phase, preferably through formal sign-off by the project sponsor?* *If no, decide what conditions need to be met to get authorization and begin to meet them.*

*See Action Item: Close Out Project Activities for a sample sign-off form.

WHAT A VETERAN PROJECT MANAGER MIGHT DO

A veteran project manager working on a large or complex project might obtain sign-off (written approval) of each deliverable, in addition to obtaining approval of the project phase.

No matter what the project size or complexity, the project manager should obtain adequate, formal authorization and support to execute each phase.

Pitfalls and Cautions

The new project manager, eager to show initiative, might want to move from one project phase to the next with nothing more than verbal approval. This is risky, since the project manager is assuming the authority to expend the organization's valuable resources.

Ask yourself: "If I start this phase without written authorization, who will back me up if we run into problems?"

Always get written approval to begin a project phase, and make sure you have adequate authority to make job assignments, spend money, use equipment, and so on. Otherwise, you may find yourself all alone out on a limb when problems occur.

For More Information . . .

See PMI's *PMBOK* item 5.1, Initiation.

PLANNING

Planning is of major importance on a project, because by definition, the project involves creating something unique. In other words, you may be heading into uncharted waters, so you should have a plan to help you get through them safely. (For more details, see the expanded description of this process in Part II.)

The following Action Items support the process of planning:

- Action Item: Describe Project Scope
- Action Item: Define and Sequence Project Activities
- Action Item: Estimate Durations for Activities and Resources Required
- Action Item: Develop a Project Schedule
- Action Item: Estimate Costs
- Action Item: Build a Budget and Spending Plan
- Optional Action Item: Create a Formal Quality Plan
- Optional Action Item: Create a Formal Project Communications Plan
- Action Item: Organize and Acquire Staff
- Optional Action Item: Identify Risks and Plan to Respond
- Optional Action Item: Plan for and Acquire Outside Resources
- Action Item: Organize the Project Plan
- Action Item: Close Out the Project Planning Phase
- Action Item: Revisit the Project Plan and Replan if Needed

ACTION ITEM: DESCRIBE PROJECT SCOPE

ASSIGNMENT

Create an adequate description of project scope.

DESIRED OUTPUTS

- Statement of project scope, to include:[9]
  —Project justification
  —List of major project deliverables
  —List of project objectives (quantifiable criteria that must be met for success—at a minimum, cost, schedule, and quality measures)
- Scope management plan, to include:[10]
  —How scope will be managed (i.e., how scope changes will be identified and integrated into the project)
  —Expected stability of the project
- Work breakdown structure—a "family tree" that organizes and defines the total scope of the project[11]

BACKGROUND INFORMATION

Project scope refers to the sum of all products (deliverables) and services to be provided by the project. In order to manage the scope of the project, you must be able to describe all the work activities and deliverables that are included in the project. In addition, you must be able to distinguish these from activities and deliverables that are not part of the project but that stakeholders might later decide would be "nice to have."

The formal description of project scope, presented as part of the project plan, makes the boundaries of the project clear. This description includes details about the project objectives, the work product (deliverables), and the amount of time and resources that will be consumed on the project. In addition, the description of scope should describe what actions you will take when some aspect of the scope changes. (For example, how will you handle special requests for work products that are not planned? How will you handle exceptions? Will you issue a contract change order to change the scope formally?)

To develop a detailed description of project scope, you might want to try building a work breakdown structure. A work breakdown structure (WBS) describes the components and subcomponents of the project's various work products as a "family tree."[12] Consider this example. A couple has decided that they would like to change their lifestyle by moving to their own custom-made log cabin in the wilderness. Figure 4 shows the WBS for this project.

Note that the figure shows *all* the various outputs that must be created, not just

Figure 4. Work breakdown structure chart.

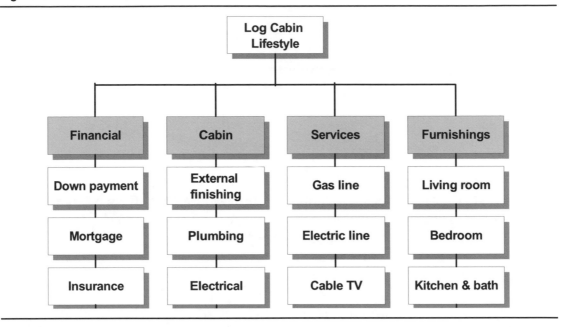

the most obvious. We can see, for example, that getting the financing arranged and the services installed will be important project outcomes, so the couple must account for these in their plans. Had they focused only on the most obvious (the cabin's construction), they may have overlooked these outcomes.

Now consider the next example. The team responsible for Project X has identified five phases into which they might cluster all of their various project deliverables: Need and Feasibility, Project Plan, Deliverables' Specifications, Deliverables, and Testing and Implementation (see Figure 5). Within each of these phases we can see many *finished deliverables* (such as prototypes and approved deliverables) and also many *interim deliverables* (such as the project charter, flowcharts, reviews, revisions, formal approvals, and test strategies).

Note: In both of these WBS examples, all of the items are expressed as *nouns*. As such, they are measurable, tangible targets or work products that the team must strive to generate. (In the next Action Item in this handbook, Define and Sequence Project Activities, we will focus on identifying all the tasks necessary to generate each of these project deliverables. These tasks, because they represent specific actions which the team must take, will be expressed as *verbs*.)

As these examples show, a main benefit of starting a project with a WBS is that it keeps the project manager focused on uncovering all the hidden deliverables. Only after all these specific outputs are examined in detail can the project manager build an accurate list of activities (i.e., the project work tasks) necessary to create these deliverables.

Decomposition involves breaking down the project deliverables into smaller, more manageable components. This typically involves three steps:[13]

Figure 5. Project X: Phased work breakdown structure chart.

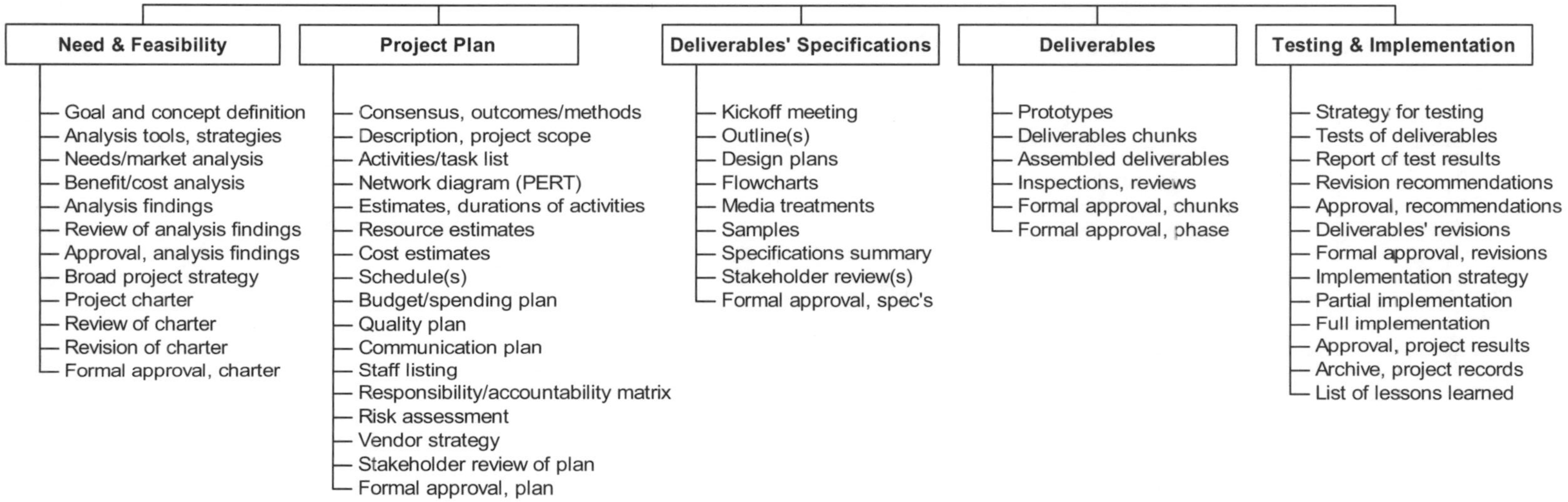

Need & Feasibility
- Goal and concept definition
- Analysis tools, strategies
- Needs/market analysis
- Benefit/cost analysis
- Analysis findings
- Review of analysis findings
- Approval, analysis findings
- Broad project strategy
- Project charter
- Review of charter
- Revision of charter
- Formal approval, charter

Project Plan
- Consensus, outcomes/methods
- Description, project scope
- Activities/task list
- Network diagram (PERT)
- Estimates, durations of activities
- Resource estimates
- Cost estimates
- Schedule(s)
- Budget/spending plan
- Quality plan
- Communication plan
- Staff listing
- Responsibility/accountability matrix
- Risk assessment
- Vendor strategy
- Stakeholder review of plan
- Formal approval, plan

Deliverables' Specifications
- Kickoff meeting
- Outline(s)
- Design plans
- Flowcharts
- Media treatments
- Samples
- Specifications summary
- Stakeholder review(s)
- Formal approval, spec's

Deliverables
- Prototypes
- Deliverables chunks
- Assembled deliverables
- Inspections, reviews
- Formal approval, chunks
- Formal approval, phase

Testing & Implementation
- Strategy for testing
- Tests of deliverables
- Report of test results
- Revision recommendations
- Approval, recommendations
- Deliverables' revisions
- Formal approval, revisions
- Implementation strategy
- Partial implementation
- Full implementation
- Approval, project results
- Archive, project records
- List of lessons learned

Step 1. Identify major project elements (both deliverables and project management components). For example, some deliverable-related project elements might include software design specifications or blueprints for a building, while project management–related elements might include status reports and product review meetings.

Step 2. Make a list of project elements, and organize them into related groups.

Step 3. Decide if the project elements are described at an adequate level of detail to allow you to make cost estimates for each and estimates of time required to build or work with each element.

CHECKLIST: Evaluating Project Scope

Instructions: This checklist is designed to help you evaluate your description of project scope.[14] Gather together all information (rough notes, memos, and so forth) relating to project scope; then, using the list below, check off the items that you have completed.

If you are working with a formal or informal advisory group, you might ask all of its members to work through this checklist with you.

- There is a clear project justification (i.e., a clear explanation of why the project has been undertaken).
- There is a list of all major project deliverables.
- There is a list of project objectives.
- The project objective list includes quantifiable criteria for success, including:
  —Cost criteria (i.e., What cost limits will be met in order for the project to be judged a success?)
  —Schedule criteria (i.e., What calendar dates will be met in order for the project to be judged a success?)
  —Quality measures (i.e., By what measures will we know that the project has produced quality deliverables or achieved quality results?)
- Project objectives do *not* take the form of fuzzy descriptions such as "to provide maximum customer satisfaction" or "to create state-of-the-art deliverables."
- There is a description of what constitutes an out-of-bound condition that could lead to a change in project scope (e.g., excess costs, schedule extensions, reduction in quality, increase in deliverables).
- There is a description of what to do when project scope changes are identified (e.g., notify sponsor, execute a contract change order, stop project work).
- There is a description of the expected stability of the project (e.g., "We have anticipated and spelled out potential unstable factors").
- There is a work breakdown structure (WBS) or a "family tree" chart that organizes and defines the total scope of the project.
- All the items above have been organized into a single, comprehensive document.

WORKSHEET: Project Scope Statement

Project Name: _____   **Date:** _____

Project Manager: _____

Project Tracking Number: _____

Project Justification (problem or opportunity addressed):

Overview of Deliverables (broad brush only; place detailed WBS in appendixes—for example: needs analysis/feasibility study notes, detailed WBS, preliminary schedule, preliminary cost estimate, sample deliverables, background memos/reports, organization chart of project team

Specific Project Objectives & Success Criteria (schedule, cost, quality):

Scope Management Issues (including ways scope changes will be handled and contract change orders will be processed:

Primary Stakeholders and Roles (including broad statement of roles and responsibilities of all customers, sponsors, contributors, reviewers, managers, sign-off authorities, project manager):

Key Assumptions (including broad statement of sponsor and stakeholder inputs and resources to be provided, as well as what activities and deliverables lie outside the project scope):

Signatures: The following people agree that the above information is accurate:

- Project team members:

- Project sponsor and authorizing managers:

WHAT A VETERAN PROJECT MANAGER MIGHT DO

A project management professional might undertake some of these activities to clarify project scope:[15]

- *Enlist expert support.* Use his or her professional network to help identify subject-matter experts in a particular field, then work with these experts to identify alternatives and assess them.
- *Conduct product analysis.* Analyze the product (deliverables) of the project in detail using such methods as systems engineering, value engineering, and value analysis.
- *Conduct benefit-cost analysis.* Estimate tangible and intangible costs and benefits of various project alternatives and then consider the return on investment.
- *Identify alternatives.* Use brainstorming, mind-mapping, or other techniques to come up with project alternatives.

PITFALLS AND CAUTIONS

The "little details" that you fail to include in your project scope statement can add up to substantial cost overruns and schedule extensions. Yet novice project managers are often tempted to define project scope in somewhat broad or even vague terms. Don't fall victim to this temptation.

Actively try to visualize each phase of the project so that you see in your mind's eye as many project events and deliverables as you possibly can. Talk to project veterans about what kinds of unforeseen project deliverables might be needed. And ask these veterans to evaluate your project plans to identify potential problems or scope elements you have failed to include.

A few extra hours spent defining scope accurately in the first place can help you avoid weeks of rework and the frustration or embarrassment of exceeding your schedule and budget.

FOR MORE INFORMATION . . .

See PMI's *PMBOK* item 5.2, Scope Planning, and item 5.3, Scope Definition.

ACTION ITEM: DEFINE AND SEQUENCE PROJECT ACTIVITIES

ASSIGNMENT

Define and sequence all the activities necessary to complete the project.

DESIRED OUTPUTS

- An activity list (list of all activities that will be performed on the project)
- Updates of the work breakdown structure (WBS) (for details, see Action Item: Describe Project Scope)
- A project network diagram showing the relationships among project activities

BACKGROUND INFORMATION

The description of project scope already developed included a description of project deliverables, probably in the form of a WBS. Now it's time to build on this description by identifying all the specific activities that must be performed to produce the various project deliverables. After these activities are identified, you can show how they relate to one another. In particular, you need to show which activities must precede others, which can be performed in parallel, which activities may be grouped in clusters, and so on.

Note that it is unnecessary to identify how long each activity will take (i.e., its duration) at this time. We will estimate duration later.

In order to define activities, you will need the following information:

- Description of project scope (created earlier)
- Historical data on the kinds of activities that were required for previous similar projects

The process of defining activities involves breaking down a preliminary list of activities into more detailed activities (see the description of decomposition in the preceding Action Item).[16] In order to sequence activities, you will need the following information:

- Detailed description of the deliverables to be created. This will help you determine the actions required to create the deliverables.
- Detailed list of activities.
- Dependencies regarding project activities. This simply means asking yourself, "Which project activities *depend on* other project activities in order to be completed?" or "Which project activities *depend on* external events in order to be completed?" Here are some different types of dependencies:[17]
  —Mandatory dependencies—awareness of which activities absolutely depend

on the completion of other activities. For example, you must lay the foundation before you erect the walls of a house.

—Discretionary dependencies—awareness of professional "best practices" regarding the sequencing of activities in a particular profession. For example, film producers often create a script before they hire actors; however, these activities may be completed in reverse order, at the producer's discretion.

—External dependencies—awareness of factors outside the project that may affect the sequence or scheduling of activities. For example, the prototype of the product is needed in time for a trade show, or the government requires that certain financial information be accumulated and reported at a certain time in the project.

—Leads and lags—awareness of ways in which a particular project activity must be delayed (creating lag time) or can be started before its successor activity is completed (allowing lead time).[18] (See Figure 6.) ***Caution:*** Lead time and lag time should be carefully analyzed in order to rule out the possibility that the lead or lag can be eliminated. Find out exactly what is causing the leads or lags and make sure each lead or lag is justified.

When you have figured out all of the task relationships, you are ready to organize them into a network diagram.[19] Such a diagram can highlight important relationships among project activities, allowing project planners to analyze these relationships and, if necessary, change them. Figure 7 shows two different types of network diagrams, both illustrating a do-it-yourself kitchen remodeling project. The kitchen owner has decided to repaint the walls, regrout the tile on the countertop, and install some new appliances. Note how the progress from one project activity to another can easily be seen in the diagrams.

The diagrams also show which activities are dependent on others. For example, it's easy to see that if the activity "buy paint and grouting tools" becomes delayed,

Figure 6. Project network diagram.

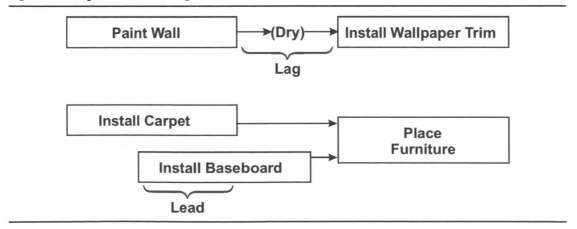

Figure 7. Network diagrams for kitchen remodeling project.

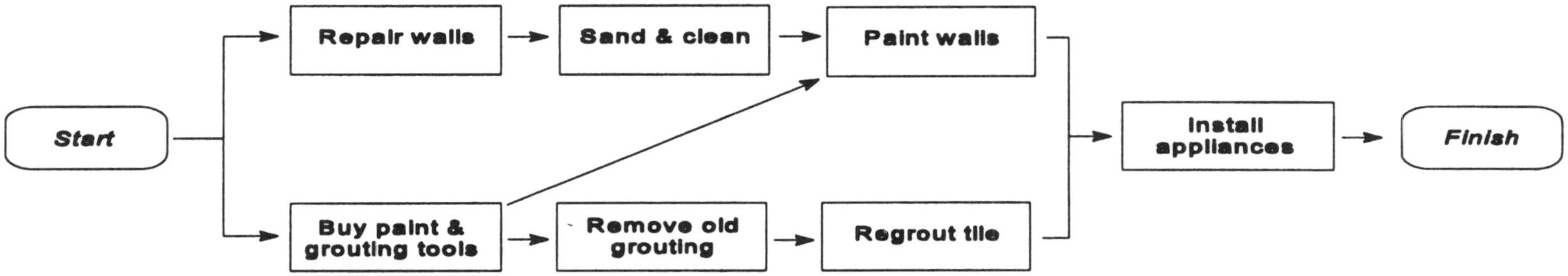

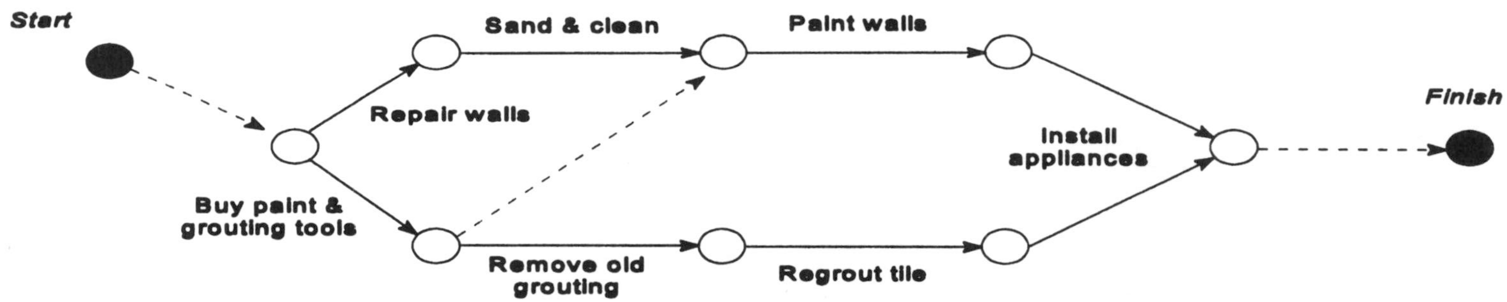

there will be a corresponding delay in "paint walls," since these activities are tied together.

In addition to highlighting important relationships among project activities, a network diagram can also help project planners find the *critical path*: the series of project activities that are inextricably linked and will take the longest time to complete. Once this critical path is identified, project managers must pay special attention to each of the activities on it, since any activities that cause the critical path to be extended will lengthen the entire project schedule. On the other hand, if critical path activities can be accelerated, then the entire project schedule can be accelerated.

As you can see, a network diagram can be an important communication tool, allowing the project manager to discuss with stakeholders the relationships among project activities. In this way, stakeholders can evaluate different options and help the project manager fine-tune project activities.

Guidelines for Defining and Sequencing Project Activities

Instructions: Follow these steps to define and sequence your project activities. You may use the check boxes to mark the items as completed.

If you are working with a formal or informal advisory group, you might ask its members to work through these guidelines with you.

Step 1: Assemble the following:

- Description of project scope
- Historical data on activities required for similar projects (i.e., What activities are usually completed for similar types of projects?)
- One or more experts who have defined and sequenced activities for similar projects

Step 2: Create detailed activities lists. (Consider conducting brainstorming sessions with key stakeholders.)

- Examine the WBS, and for each product (deliverable) to be created, make a list of specific activities.
- Group these activities into clusters or groups of related activities.
- Separate some of the clustered activities into activities that may stand alone.

Step 3: Create the project network diagram.

- Draw a diagram showing the relationships among activities (which must come first, which must come next, which ones may proceed at the same time, and so on).

Step 4: Evaluate the detailed list of activities and the network diagram, and revise or adjust as needed.

- Revisit your network diagram and list of activities, and decide if they can be refined.
- Ask an outside adviser (an expert in the project activities) to evaluate your network diagram and supporting activity list.
- Consider expanding or adding a level of detail to all activities whose measures of quality, cost, or schedule are unclear.

WHAT A VETERAN PROJECT MANAGER MIGHT DO

A project management professional might employ one or more of these techniques to analyze and sequence project activities:[20]

- *Enlisting Expert Support.* Use his or her professional network to help identify subject-matter experts in a particular field. Then work with these experts to define and sequence project activities.
- *Precedence Diagramming Method (PDM).* This is a method of constructing a project network diagram by using nodes (boxes) to represent activities and connecting them with arrows to show dependencies (illustrated in the top half of Figure 7, this is sometimes called AON, or activity on node).
- *Arrow Diagramming Method (ADM).* This is a method of constructing a project network diagram using arrows to represent the activities and connecting them at nodes to show dependencies (illustrated in the bottom half of Figure 7, this is sometimes called AOA, or activity on arrow).
- *Conditional Diagramming Methods* (such as GERT, or graphical evaluation and review technique) that allow for "loops" or repeated series of activities
- *Network templates.* Use standardized networks of activities for portions of the project.
- *Project Management or Flowcharting Software* to allow easy construction and editing of network diagrams.

PITFALLS AND CAUTIONS

Novice project managers might be tempted to depict all project tasks as purely sequential and linear. However, much time and money can be saved by creating a plan that has several activities happening at the same time. On the other hand, in an attempt to get things done quickly, a novice project manager might try to create a plan that has too many project activities going on at the same time. This may cause confusion or bottlenecks as people and other resources are expected to do several things at once.

It's difficult to figure out exactly which project activities may be sequenced in a linear fashion and which may occur simultaneously. In fact, figuring this out is an art that is best performed by a veteran in the field. If you are a newcomer to the field you are managing or if you are working with complex task specialties, be sure to work with experienced veterans when you define and sequence tasks. Also, as we cautioned in the preceding Action Item, make sure to break down the activities into as much detail as you possibly can, so that you will avoid having to complete unforeseen project activities and incurring cost or schedule overruns.

For More Information . . .

See PMI's *PMBOK* item 6.1, Activity Definition, and item 6.2, Activity Sequencing.

Action Item: Estimate Durations for Activities and Resources Required

Assignment

Estimate durations for activities and resources required to complete those activities.

Desired Outputs

Estimate of durations (time required) for each activity, and assumptions related to each estimate

Statement of resource requirements (the people, equipment, and materials needed for each activity)

Updates of activity list (how the activities list will need to be modified now that we have looked at durations and resources in greater detail)

Background Information

Duration estimates are quantitative assessments of the likely number of work periods that will be required to complete an activity.[21] In other words, how long (in hours, days, weeks) will it take to perform the activity?

Resources are defined as any people, equipment, and materials needed to execute a project.[22] Resources may take all sorts of forms, depending on the needs of the project and the industry in which the project is executed. For example, human resources include any suppliers, contractors, or vendors, as well as all manner of professionals, craftspeople, and other specialists. Equipment resources can include such things as construction cranes, computers, copying machines, and media production equipment. And materials can take forms as divergent as lumber, office supplies, computer disks, or photographic film. Resources may be salaried, rented by the hour, or purchased outright.

A statement of resource requirements outlines specifically what categories of workers (as opposed to particular people), what types of equipment, and what kinds of materials will be needed to complete each activity.[23]

Sometimes it's possible to shorten the duration of an activity by assigning more resources. For example, by making three roofers available instead of one, it may be possible to cover a roof with shingles in one-third the time. This, in turn, could mean that you will need to acquire extra equipment or materials to accommodate all the roofers. Also, putting more people on the project could mean increased training costs or more complicated communications requirements. The project manager must consider the trade-offs.

Because estimates of duration are so closely linked to the resources that will be used, it's often the case that we consider these together during project planning.

Project Effort versus Duration

Effort is the number of labor units (staff hours, days, or weeks) required to complete a particular project task or activity. In contrast, *duration* is the period of time over which a project task or activity takes place. When we total up all the effort (e.g., labor hours) for a particular job category such as programmers or bricklayers, we can then figure out how many people we will need on a job and how much these people will cost if we pay them a certain hourly rate.

Duration is determined by examining effort and other factors that aren't labor related, such as time required for cement to harden or for a committee to review and approve design specifications. Because an accurate project schedule must take into consideration anything that consumes time, whether it is labor related or not, the duration estimate is used to establish the schedule for the project.

For example, let's say it takes one person 3 hours to paint a room and an additional 4 hours for the paint to dry so that we can begin installing some special lighting fixtures. The task "paint the wall" would require 3 person-hours of effort. However, we would need to allow 7 hours duration (3 hours to paint plus 4 hours to dry) in our schedule before we could begin the next task, installing fixtures. Alternately, if we assigned two painters to this task, we could shorten the painting time to $1^{1}/_{2}$ hours for each person (total effort: 3 person-hours), but the walls would still require 4 hours to dry. In this way, we could reduce the duration to $5^{1}/_{2}$ hours ($1^{1}/_{2}$ hours to paint plus 4 hours to dry). In this example, the ultimate cost of the task, since it is based on 3 person-hours of labor, will remain the same whether we use one or two painters. However, the duration required may change, based on our resource allocation strategy.

EXAMPLE: Effort/Duration Table

Phase, Activity, or Task	*Resource: Writer Effort:*	*Resource: Technical Subject-Matter Expert (SME) Effort:*	*Resource: Client Reviewer Effort:*	*Resource: Research Computer Effort:*	*Duration:*
Discuss requirements	1 hour	1 hour	1 hour	—	1 hour
Develop outline	8 hours	3 hours	—	4 hours	8 hours
Review outline	—	—	1 hour	—	8 hours
Obtain client feedback and approval	1 hour	1 hour	1 hour	—	1 hour
Write first draft	24 hours	8 hours	—	2 hours	24 hours
Review draft	—	—	3 hours	—	40 hours
Obtain client feedback and approval	3 hours	3 hours	3 hours	—	3 hours
Revise and finalize	6 hours	1 hour	—	1 hour	6 hours
Totals	43 hours	17 hours	9 hours	7 hours	91 hours

The Example: Effort/Duration Table shown here for a small writing project reflects the following work process:

1. *Discuss requirements.* The writer, the technical subject-matter expert (SME), and the client will meet for 1 hour to discuss the project requirements.
2. *Develop outline.* The writer will be working for about 8 hours developing the outline, with some support (estimated at 3 hours) from the SME. They are estimating that they will need the research computer for about 4 hours total. The client will not be involved.
3. *Review outline.* The client has asked that she be allowed to set aside a day (8 hours) for reviewing the outline. Sometime during that allocated day, the client will spend an hour doing the review.
4. *Obtain client feedback and approval.* Everyone will meet for 1 hour to obtain and interpret client feedback on the outline and get the client's approval to move on.
5. *Write first draft.* The writer will spend about 3 workdays (24 total hours) creating the draft. The technical SME will be reviewing and providing feedback along the way (8 hours). The research computer is estimated to be needed for 2 hours.
6. *Review draft.* The client has asked that she be allowed to set aside a week (40 hours) for reviewing the draft (see duration). Sometime during that allocated week, the client will spend 3 hours doing the review.
7. *Obtain client feedback and approval.* Everyone will meet for 3 hours to obtain and interpret client feedback on the outline and get the client's approval to move on.
8. *Revise and finalize.* The writer will spend about 6 hours making revisions based on the client's feedback and then finalize the document. The SME is allocated up to 1 hour to help the writer.

Completing this table achieves several powerful benefits:

- We clarify our thinking about activities/tasks and the time required to complete them.
- We begin to see which resources we need and exactly when we need them.
- We are able to make more refined requests for support resources and for client-sponsor participation. (That is, instead of saying, "We need your help on a six-month project," we can say, "We need you for a few hours on task A and a few hours on task B.")
- We have assembled "duration" information to help us build our schedule.
- We have assembled "effort" information to help us build our estimate of the costs of people assigned to the project.

In order to estimate durations and resources, you will need this information:[24]

- Scope statement
- Activity list and network diagram
- Description of the resource pool, including resources available and their capabilities
- Information on similar, previous activities from project files, commercial databases, and project team knowledge
- Organizational policy regarding staffing, rental or purchase of equipment and supplies, and so on

Guidelines for Estimating Durations for Activities and Resources Required

Instructions: Follow these steps to estimate the durations for project activities and the resources required. You may use the check boxes to mark items as completed.

If you are working with a formal or informal advisory group, you might ask its members to work through this worksheet with you.

Step 1: Assemble the following:

- Scope statement
- Activity list and network diagram
- Description of the resource pool, including resources available and their capabilities
- Historical data on similar activities from project files, commercial databases, or project team knowledge
- Organizational policy regarding staffing, rental or purchase of equipment and supplies, and so forth
- One or more experts who have estimated durations and resources required for similar projects

Step 2: Examine each activity; then estimate its duration and probable resources required.

- Estimate of duration for each activity
- Estimate of resources required and corresponding effort for each activity
- Assumptions about the resources to be assigned (for example, employees will need to work 10-hour days or the machine will need to process 75 units per hour)

  Note: Some organizations can supply you with data on what can reasonably be expected from a particular resource in order to achieve a quality work product. For example, a reasonable expectation for a veteran bricklayer might be to lay *X* number of bricks per day. If the project manager is forced, due to budget cuts, to hire fewer bricklayers or inexperienced bricklayers, then you may not be able to maintain your project schedule. Your assumptions should clearly state any "reasonable expectancies" such as these so that they may be captured in your project plan.

Step 3: Reevaluate the activity relationships, given your duration and resource assumptions.

- Examine clusters or groups of related activities.
- Examine stand-alone activities.

Step 4: Adjust the project network diagram as needed.

- Network diagram adjusted

Step 5: Informally present your estimates of durations and resources required to an expert colleague to "reality-check" it; adjust as needed.

- Expert review, adjustment

WORKSHEET: Estimating Durations, Resources, and Effort

Instructions: In the far left column, enter the project phase, activity, or task for which you wish to estimate the effort and duration. In the blank spaces at the top, name the resources you will need to complete these activities. In the columns under "Effort," list the amount of labor hours or days that resources will likely consume completing their portion of each activity. In the far right column, enter the duration (period of time over which the activity will take place) for each activity. Finally, total each column to come up with a summary estimate of each resource's effort and overall project duration. Refer to the example Effort/Duration Table for guidance.

Phase, Activity, or Task	Resource: _____ Effort	Resource: _____ Effort	Resource: _____ Effort	Resource: _____ Effort	Duration

Phase, Activity, or Task	Resource: ___ Effort	Resource: ___ Effort	Resource: ___ Effort	Resource: ___ Effort	Duration
Totals					

What a Veteran Project Manager Might Do

A veteran project manager might use his or her professional network to help identify subject-matter experts in a particular field, then work with these experts to create realistic duration estimates of the activities.

A veteran project manager might also include some estimate of probability regarding the accuracy of his or her duration estimates. For example, he might say that a given activity will take two weeks, plus or minus two days. Or she might say that there is a 15 percent probability of exceeding the two-week period, which means there is an 85 percent chance that the activity will take less than two weeks.[25]

If there is confusion or controversy regarding the estimates of a particular set of activities, the veteran project manager might take the time to flesh out that set of activities by expanding their description to a greater level of detail. By this deeper analysis, it is typically possible to identify and discuss assumptions, thereby clearing up the confusion or settling the controversy.

Pitfalls and Cautions

As a novice project manager, you might be tempted to estimate the durations of activities without consulting peers and experts. Even if you are yourself an expert in all of the activities required, this is foolhardy! Take the time to have others review your estimates. In fact, there is no shame in pulling together a team of experienced people in a brainstorming session to work through your entire list of project activities and assign durations. If you are able to include key members of the project team in the session, you may receive as an added benefit their strong commitment to live up to the duration estimates. After all, the members themselves would be making the estimates!

In addition, it's critical to document assumptions you are making about resources and durations. For example, if you are assuming only part-time employees will work on a particular project activity, then it's crucial that this assumption be captured in writing so that someone evaluating the schedule can see why this activity might take longer to complete than others. Other types of assumptions worth documenting here include:

- Experience level of the workers assigned (old hands may work faster than rookies).
- Brand names of equipment to be leased or purchased to perform the project (some equipment may be harder to use, and therefore extend the duration required).
- Decision-making speed. For example, those reviewing deliverables will make decisions in two days, not three weeks.

The bottom line: Document any assumptions about the quality or quantity of your resources that makes them uniquely able to perform the task in the duration you estimate. In this way, if stakeholders try to substitute resources (to save money, for example), they will need to provide ones that can perform to the same specifications.

FOR MORE INFORMATION . . .

See PMI's *PMBOK* item 6.3, Activity Duration Estimating, and item 7.1, Resource Planning.

ACTION ITEM: DEVELOP A PROJECT SCHEDULE

ASSIGNMENT

Develop a project schedule.

DESIRED OUTPUTS

- Project schedule (planned start-and-finish dates for each activity) in the form of Gantt charts, network diagrams, milestone charts, or text tables
- Supporting details, as required, to show resource usage over time, cash flow projections over time, order and delivery schedules, or other schedule-related details
- Schedule management plan describing how schedule changes will be handled

BACKGROUND INFORMATION

Developing a schedule means determining planned start-and-finish dates for each activity.[26]

After you have identified project activities and established how long each should take, it is possible to connect them to actual calendar dates. These may then be displayed as Gantt charts, network diagrams, milestone charts, or text tables.

A *Gantt chart* is a graphic display of schedule-related information. In the typical Gantt chart, activities are listed down the left side of the chart, dates are shown across the top or bottom, and planned activity durations are shown as horizontal bars, placed according to the dates. A Gantt chart is sometimes called a *bar chart*. Because the Gantt bars are proportionally longer for project activities that take longer to complete, Gantt charts can effectively display relative differences in durations of activities.

Choose a Gantt chart when you want to show which activities will take longer than others. Note that project management software packages create high-quality Gantt charts quickly and easily. A sample of a Gantt chart is shown in Figure 8.

Figure 8. Sample Gantt chart.

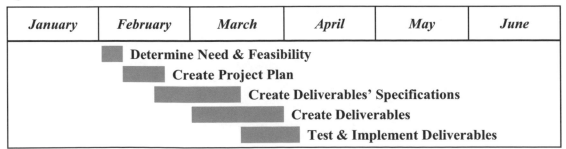

A *network diagram,* as discussed in Action Item: Define and Sequence Project Activities, shows which project activities depend on which other activities in order to be completed. Choose a network diagram when you want to show the relationships among activities clearly. Network diagrams may be presented with schedule data included on each activity description, as shown in Figure 9.[27]

In addition, network diagrams may be time-scaled to show the relative amount of time passing between activities.[28] In the example in Figure 10, we not only see the relative length of time to be spent on each activity, but we have identified a delay or period of downtime between regrouting the tile and installing the appliances.

Milestone charts show only the most significant project events. Choose a milestone chart when you want to provide broad overviews of the project's main events for executive audiences or others who want to see only the big picture.[29] Figure 11 is an example of a milestone chart. In addition, project events and dates may be presented as *text tables,* as shown in Figure 12.

Finally, since everyone is familiar with its format, an *ordinary calendar* can be a powerful way to communicate the project schedule. As Figure 13 illustrates, a calendar can show relative duration and concurrence of activities, as well as days of the week and month, including weekends.

You should select your schedule format carefully with the needs of the audience in mind. Ask yourself:

- Who are the readers of this schedule?
- How much information do they need (big picture or details?)
- What form of schedule do these readers like (or expect) to see?
- Should I create customized versions of the schedule for certain audiences, certain activities or phases, or certain display purposes?

Note: Project management software can be extremely valuable in helping you automatically generate customized versions of the same project's schedule. For example, the same project plan may be displayed as a Gantt chart, a text table, and a network diagram, and the plan may be filtered so that the schedule shows only those project activities relevant to a particular person, project phase, or time period.

When you have answered the questions above, you are ready to build your schedule. The following guidelines can help.

Guidelines for Developing the Project Schedule

Instructions: Follow these steps to develop a project schedule. You may use the check boxes to mark items as completed.

If you are working with a formal or informal advisory group, you might ask its members to work through these guidelines with you.

(text continues on page 67)

Figure 9. Network diagram with schedule data.

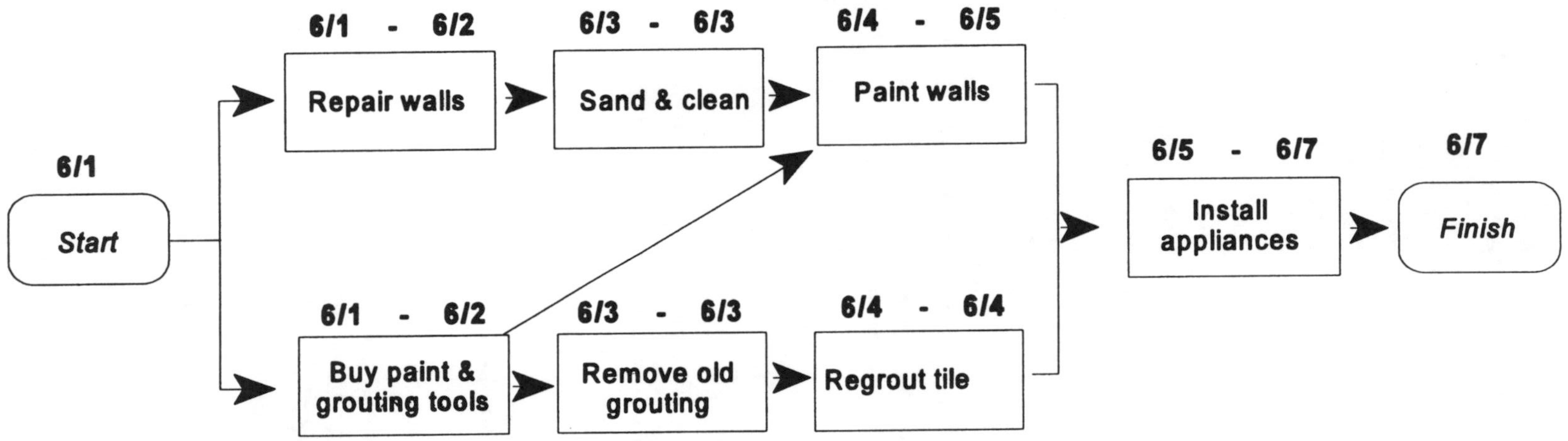

Figure 10. Network diagram with time scale.

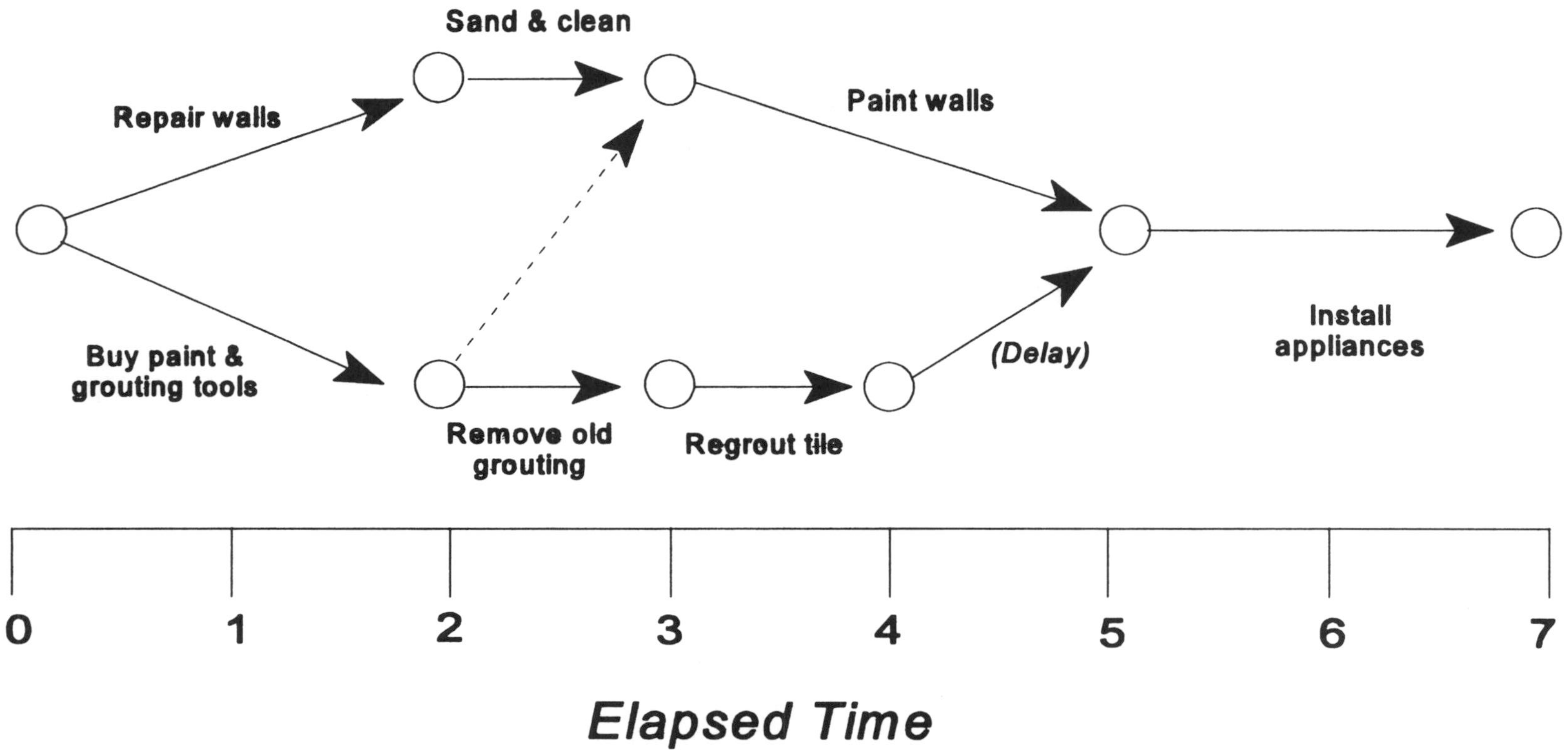

Figure 11. Sample milestone chart.

Task Name	February	March	April	May	June
Feasibility Study Complete	3/1 ▲ Feasibility Study Complete				
Project Plan Complete	3/15 ▲ Project Plan Complete				
Blueprint Complete	4/1 ▲ Blueprint Complete				
Utilities Connected	4/15 ▲ Utilities Connected				
Cabin Frame Complete	5/1 ▲ Cabin Frame Complete				
Interior Finish Complete	5/15 ▲ Interior Finished				
Move In	6/3 ▲ Move In				

Figure 12. Sample text table.

Date	Activity
Jan. 15–Mar. 15	Conduct research
Mar. 16–Apr. 16	Create detailed deliverables' specifications
Apr. 16–Apr. 26	Sponsor review of detailed deliverables' specifications

Figure 13. Sample calendar.

SUN	MON	TUE	WED	THUR	FRI	SAT
1	2 * Repair walls * Buy paint	3 * Sand, etc.	4 * Paint walls * Regrout tile	5	6 * Install appliances	7
8	9 * Shop around for new game room components ⟶	10	11	12	13	14
15 ⟶	16	17	18	19	20 * Design new game room	21
22	23	24	25	26	27	28
29	30	31				

Step 1: Assemble the following:[30]

- Your estimates of duration and resources required
- Information about availability of resources—how many will be available and when
- Organization calendars—showing when work is allowed (when resources will be available, which days are holidays, which days are vacation days, and so on)
- Project constraints, including:
  —Imposed dates based on stakeholder requirements, seasonal weather, and so forth
  —Key events or major milestone completion dates
  —Unusual assumptions about resources or durations
- A blank calendar or other blank form on which to record the schedule

Step 2: On the blank calendar, label any holidays or other dates when resources won't be available.

- Identify holidays, vacations, and the like.

Step 3: Examine each activity and its duration, and plot the activity on the calendar. On a separate page labeled "Assumptions," capture any assumptions about the activity, including assumptions about the resources to be assigned.

- Plot activities, durations.
- List assumptions about resources.

Step 4: After the days are plotted on a standard calendar, create other types of schedule displays that will be useful (e.g., Gantt charts, network diagrams, milestone charts, text tables).

- Create specialized project-wide charts, schedules.

Step 5: If your project's network diagram or Gantt chart shows many different activities happening at the same time, consider finding the *critical path*—the sequence of activities that takes the most time to complete—and attempting to shorten it in order to reduce the project's overall duration.

Here are some ways you can shorten the critical path:

- *Reduce the duration* of some of the activities. (Simply allow less time for them.)
- *Add more resources* to some of the activities. (If you assign more people or equipment, you can often reduce the time required. Be careful, however, since this can increase the coordination time required.)
- *Allow more hours* in the workday. (Allow for overtime or add another shift.)
- *Allow more workdays* in the schedule. (Allow for weekend or holiday work.)
- *Change the relationships of activities*. (Instead of performing some tasks sequentially, one at a time, perform them at the same time, in parallel fashion.)
- *Use slack time more effectively*. (Find slack between activities or downtime for some resources, and move up or plan to complete pending activities during this time.)

- *Redefine one or more project phases*. (Check to see if some activities contained within a phase are causing the phase to be delayed needlessly; then consider moving these activities to the next phase.)
- *Redefine "done."* (Consider whether some deliverables, particularly interim deliverables such as blueprints, prototypes, or drafts, might be defined as "finished" in a less complete form.)
- *Reduce the amount of deliverables* that a particular activity produces. (It takes less time to do less work!)
- *Reduce the overall project scope*. (Eliminate some work products, processes, or deliverables.)

Caution: After you have determined which of the methods you would like to use to shorten the critical path, you should discuss them with your sponsors or stakeholders. Since many of these methods result in fundamental changes in project structure, you should discuss the positive and negative effects they might have on the project, and obtain sponsor or stakeholder approval.

Step 6: Consider making customized activity schedules. They could be tailored for executive overview, for individual categories of resources (e.g., electricians, carpenters, landscapers), or for special project teams (workers in Argentina, in England, in France).

- Consider creating or create customized schedules.

Step 7: Informally present your preliminary schedules to an expert colleague to "reality-check" it; adjust as needed.

- Reality-check with a peer or expert.

WHAT A VETERAN PROJECT MANAGER MIGHT DO

A project management professional might use one or more of these techniques to create, analyze, and then recreate the project schedule:[31]

- *Enlisting Expert Support.* Use his or her professional network to help identify subject-matter experts in a particular field and then work with these experts to build the project schedule.
- *Mathematical Analysis.* Calculate early and late start-and-finish dates for all project activities.
- *Duration Compression.* A special case of mathematical analysis that looks for ways to shorten the project schedule. This includes such techniques as "crashing" and "fast-tracking" (overlapping tasks).
- *Simulation.* Calculate multiple schedules with different sets of assumptions.
- *Resource Leveling.* Adjust the schedule based on uneven assignments of resources in order to level the workload of one or more overbooked resources.
- *Project Management Software.* Use such software to create "what if" scenarios

and to create many different versions of the schedule in different formats for different audiences.

PITFALLS AND CAUTIONS

A novice project manager can sometimes forget that a schedule is first and foremost a communication tool. Its purpose is to keep everyone on the project team aware of what should be going on, when. And like any other communication tool, if it isn't understandable and relevant to the audience, it is useless.

While you may breathe a sigh of relief when you finally finish that huge, complex, wall-mounted schedule, those observing it may simply scratch their heads in total confusion—and then ignore it. So expect to make lots of versions of the schedule, each based on a different user need. And plan to walk through each version in one-on-one meetings with the people who should be using it to guide their actions or whose approval (formal or informal) you will need.

Like interoffice memoranda, schedules that appear out of nowhere are likely to be ignored. So custom-tailor them, explain them, and refer to them often to keep your project on track.

FOR MORE INFORMATION . . .

See PMI's *PMBOK* item 6.4, Schedule Development.

ACTION ITEM: ESTIMATE COSTS

ASSIGNMENT

Estimate the costs of completing all project activities.

DESIRED OUTPUTS

- Cost estimates for completion of each activity
- Supporting detail, including assumptions and constraints related to costs
- Cost management plan describing how cost variances will be handled
- Revisions to the project activity list or network diagrams in response to the need for more detail about costs

BACKGROUND INFORMATION

Cost (the amount it will cost to complete the activity) should be distinguished from *price* (the amount the organization performing the activity will charge for the product or service). Pricing includes many other business factors (profit, goodwill, etc.) that aren't considered in estimating cost.

Cost estimates are quantitative assessments of the likely costs of the resources required to complete project activities.[32] Cost estimates must cover labor, materials, supplies, and other categories such as inflation and administrative costs. These estimates are frequently refined throughout the project to reflect the additional detail available as the project deliverables unfold.[33]

There are three popular methods of cost estimating:[34]

- *Bottom-Up Estimating*—estimating the cost of individual activities and summarizing or "rolling up" these costs to determine project costs
- *Analogous Estimating*—sometimes called "top down" estimating, which involves using the actual cost of a previous, similar project to make an estimate of costs for a planned project
  Caution: Project managers should be sure to challenge the assumption that the previous analogous project was actually similar to the project they are planning. It must be truly similar in order for the cost estimates to be accurate.
- *Fixed Budget Estimating*—taking the total amount of money available for the project and dividing it across the various project components to see what you can and can't afford

In order to estimate costs you will need this information:[35]

- Description of resource requirements
- Description of resource rates

- Duration estimates
- Historical data regarding costs of activities, resources, and projects
- Chart of accounts, indicating how costs should be assigned to particular accounts

There are no accepted standards for describing the accuracy of a cost estimate.[36] Therefore, project planners use all sorts of expressions of accuracy, such as these:

- "There is a 15 percent probability of exceeding $100,000." This means there is a high probability (85 percent) that the cost will not be exceeded.
- "The cost is $10,000, plus or minus $1,000." This means the activity will cost no less than $9,000 and no more than $11,000.

Note: In some organizations, while there may not be hard and fast standards for measuring the accuracy of a cost estimate, there may be opinions or critical norms. The novice project manager should check with his or her peers or supervisors to see if these can be identified.

Sample Cost-Estimation Worksheet

Figure 14 illustrates the completion of a typical worksheet for estimating project costs. In this sample, we have estimated the cost of removing brush from a vacant lot. This one-day project will involve one laborer, one truck driver/laborer, and one supervisor/laborer. In addition, we have assumed that we will need to rent a truck to carry the brush away and pay a fee at the landfill to dispose of the brush.

Note that the worksheet lists all activities, the amount of time each activity will take, and the resources to be applied to complete each activity. Note also that some resources (the workers) will incur costs based on the number of hours they take to perform the task. These are typically referred to as *variable-cost resources,* since the cost varies according to the effort expended. Other resources (like the truck and landfill dumping fee) are typically referred to as *fixed-cost resources,* since they involve a one-time cost, no matter how much effort is expended. Finally, note that the worksheet is designed to provide total costs for each resource, each activity, and the entire project.

This example is overly simplified in order to illustrate the relationship among cost elements. However, when you plan your projects, you will likely need to add many more columns for resources and break down "Miscellaneous Costs" into subcategories based on the deliverables you are creating. In addition, you should consider adding categories for contingency fees, administrative costs, profit, and other items related to your particular organization's needs.

Figure 14. Sample cost estimation worksheet: Brush removal project.

Activity	Duration	Resource Name: Laborer. Resource Rate: $10/hour. Cost of Resource for This Activity	Resource Name: Truck Driver/ Laborer. Resource Rate: $15/hour. Cost of Resource for This Activity	Resource Name: Supervisor/ Laborer. Resource Rate: $20/hour. Cost of Resource for This Activity	Miscellaneous Costs	Total Costs, Activity
Travel to site	1 hr.	$10.00	$15.00	$20.00	$150.00 (Rent truck)	$195.00
Determine strategy for clean-up	.5 hr.	$5.00	$7.50	$10.00		$22.50
Remove brush	3 hr.	$30.00	$45.00	$60.00		$135.00
Load brush in truck	1 hr.	$10.00	$15.00	$20.00		$45.00
Haul brush to landfill	.5 hr.	$5.00	$7.50	$10.00		$22.50
Unload brush at landfill	1 hr.	$10.00	$15.00	$20.00	$25.00 (Dump fee)	$70.00
Return from site	1 hr.	$10.00	$15.00	$20.00		$45.00
Return truck	.5 hr.			$10.00		$10.00
Total	8.5	$80.00	$120.00	$170.00	$175.00	$545.00

Guidelines for Making a Bottom-Up Cost Estimate

Instructions: Follow these steps to develop a project cost estimate using the bottom-up estimating technique. You may use the check boxes to mark items as completed.

If you are working with a formal or informal advisory group, you might ask some of its members to work through these guidelines with you.

Step 1: Assemble the following:

- Descriptions of all project activities
- Description of resource requirements
- Description of resource rates (e.g., how much resources will cost per hour or per day)
- Duration estimates for each activity
- Historical data regarding costs of activities, resources, and projects

Step 2: Set up a worksheet similar to that in Figure 14.

- Set up worksheet.
- Consider making a new electronic spreadsheet, using a template electronic spreadsheet file from a similar project, or using project management software to estimate the costs.

Step 3: Evaluate your worksheet according to these checkpoints:

- All project activities are listed.
- All project resources are assigned to the appropriate activities, including variable resources (paid by the hour or day) and fixed resources (paid a one-time fee).
- Costs are summarized by activity.
- Costs are summarized by resource.
- Miscellaneous fees, such as profit, standard contingencies, administrative costs, shipping, communications (fax, phone, e-mail), and other costs are considered.
- Detailed cost estimates for similar projects were consulted when building this worksheet.

Step 4: Use the worksheet to complete the cost estimate, filling in all the blanks as required.

- Complete the cost estimate.

Step 5: Informally present your preliminary cost estimate to an expert colleague to "reality-check" it; adjust as needed.

- Reality-check.

Step 6: Create summaries of costs and graphical displays of costs for presentation to stakeholders.

- Create cost summaries and graphics.

WHAT A VETERAN PROJECT MANAGER MIGHT DO

A seasoned project manager might use one or more of these techniques to estimate, analyze, and reestimate project costs:

- *Enlisting Expert Support.* Use his or her professional network to help identify subject-matter experts in a particular field and then work with these experts to estimate project costs.
- *Experimenting with Different Scenarios.* This might involve creating one scenario with minimal deliverables, minimal time frames, and minimum costs; another with maximum deliverables, maximum time frames, and maximum costs; and then a middle-of-the-road alternative to both of these. Using these

scenarios, the project manager can involve sponsors and stakeholders in discussing the merits of the different options available.

- *Project Management Software or Spreadsheet Software.* Both may be used to help with cost estimating by allowing fast yet detailed number crunching. Previous projects, if saved on disk, may be readily recalled for modification and for making fast estimates of new projects.
- *Parametric Modeling.* Any mathematical model that uses project characteristics to compute total project costs.[37]

PITFALLS AND CAUTIONS

Avoid the temptation to make "quick-and-dirty" or ballpark estimates of costs. Instead, take the time to examine methodically each project activity, its associated resources, and its costs. Actively imagine exactly what will be happening during each project event and how the money will be spent to make these things happen. And by all means examine the budget and cost estimates of projects similar to the one you are planning, since they may include line items you would otherwise overlook. Finally, be sure to note in writing any assumptions you are making about receiving cost-free contributions to your project (such as staff, equipment, or facilities) from other organizations or stakeholders. If these contributions are withheld later and you are forced to acquire these resources by purchasing them, your sponsors should not be surprised when you ask for more money.

It's this simple: You can spend time now, in the early stages of the project, making a detailed and accurate cost estimate, or you can spend time later, after the project is underway, lobbying stakeholders for more money or shortcutting key project activities because you've run short of money. It's your decision.

FOR MORE INFORMATION . . .

See PMI's *PMBOK* item 7.2, Cost Estimating.

ACTION ITEM: BUILD A BUDGET AND SPENDING PLAN

ASSIGNMENT

Build a project budget and spending plan.

DESIRED OUTPUTS

- A cost baseline or time-phased budget that will be used to measure and monitor project costs[38]
- A spending plan, telling how much will be spent on what resources at what time
- A set of procedures by which project team members will monitor costs and update the budget

BACKGROUND INFORMATION

Building a budget is simply the process of allocating the cost estimates to individual activities in order to establish a baseline for measuring project costs.

A *time-phased budget* is a budget in which cost estimates are broken out by time periods such as weeks, months, or quarters. A time-phased budget helps you figure out how much you should be spending and when; in short, it is your spending plan.

You will need the following to create a budget and spending plan:

- Project cost estimates
- Work breakdown structure (WBS)
- Project schedule

Guidelines for Building a Budget and Spending Plan

Instructions: Follow these steps to build a budget and spending plan. You may use the check boxes to mark items as completed.

If you are working with a formal or informal advisory group, you might ask some of its members to work through these guidelines with you.

Step 1: Assemble the following:

- Project cost estimates
- Work breakdown structure (WBS)
- Project schedule
- Budget forms or sample budget and spending plans approved by your organization

Step 2: Make a worksheet with headings similar to these:

Activity	Account Code	Budgeted, January	Budgeted, February	Budgeted, March	Budgeted [April, etc.]

Note: If you want to monitor your spending on a quarterly or weekly basis, then label the column headings accordingly.

■ Worksheet is completed.

Step 3: List all project activities in the left column of the worksheet.

■ Project activities are listed.

Step 4: For each activity, examine the project schedule and cost estimate to determine how much will be spent the first month, how much the second month, and so on. Then list the appropriate dollar amounts in the columns beside each activity.

■ Dollar amounts are listed by time.

Note: You might want to create a more detailed spending plan by breaking out specific resource costs under each activity. Consider this example:

Activities/Resources	Account Code	Budgeted, Jan. 1–7	Budgeted, Jan. 8–15	Budgeted, Jan. 16–23
Write script ■ Scriptwriter ■ Research assistant ■ Computer rental	PRD-5 RAS-1 EQP-1	$2,000.00 500.00 100.00	$2,000.00 — 100.00	— — 100.00
Review script ■ Producer ■ Videographer ■ Technical reviewer	PRD-1 PRD-3 EXP-1			$3,000.00 1,000.00 1,000.00
Total		$2,600.00	$2,100.00	$5,100.00

Step 5: Informally present your preliminary budget and spending plan to an expert colleague to "reality-check" it; adjust as needed based on his or her feedback.

- Budget spending plan is reality-checked and revised.

Step 6: Present your budget and spending plan to your supervisor and (if appropriate) to the sponsor; adjust as needed and obtain approval.

- Budget spending plan is approved.

WHAT A VETERAN PROJECT MANAGER MIGHT DO

A veteran project manager would likely:

- Use project management software (in which the project cost estimate has been recorded) to filter overall project costs by month, and then print out worksheets listing "Planned" versus "Actual" spending for each month. These worksheets would constitute both a budget and a spending plan.
- Examine a number of different budget and spending plans from other projects to determine the most appropriate format.
- Use his or her professional network to help identify subject-matter experts in related fields and then work with these experts to develop a budget or spending plan.

PITFALLS AND CAUTIONS

It might be tempting to avoid making a budget or spending plan, instead relying on the project cost estimate as a guide to managing your spending. But keep in mind that the cost estimate is typically not time based, but activity based, with some activities lasting many weeks or months. If you wait until an activity is completed to check on the amount of money it is consuming, you will be too late to adjust spending!

For this reason, it's better to set up a mechanism that will allow you to make frequent and regular checks on project spending. A weekly or monthly spending plan will help you make these checks quickly and easily.

FOR MORE INFORMATION . . .

See PMI's *PMBOK* item 7.3, Cost Budgeting.

OPTIONAL ACTION ITEM: CREATE A FORMAL QUALITY PLAN

ASSIGNMENT

Create a quality plan.

DESIRED OUTPUTS

- Quality management plan, including operational definitions
- Quality verification checklists
- Amendments to the project activity list, budget, and schedule to allow implementation of the quality plan

BACKGROUND INFORMATION

It has been said that quality is planned in, not inspected in. What this means is that rather than merely inspecting project outputs for conformance to quality standards, project managers should integrate quality into all project processes. And this requires substantial planning.

Quality planning is identifying which quality standards are relevant to the project and determining how to satisfy them.[39] The main benefit of managing to established quality standards is less rework, which leads to higher productivity, lower costs, and increased stakeholder satisfaction. The main cost is the expense associated with quality management activities.[40]

The following techniques support quality planning:[41]

- *Benchmarking*—comparing actual or planned practices to those of other projects in order to generate ideas for improvement.
- *Flowcharts*—showing how various project elements relate to help anticipate quality problems. Examples include the cause-and-effect diagram (sometimes called Ishikawa diagram or fishbone diagram).

To develop a quality plan, you will need information from these sources:[42]

- *Your Organization's Quality Policy.* This is defined as the overall intentions and directions of an organization with regard to quality as formally expressed by top management.
- *Scope Statement.* Since this documents the project objectives (stakeholder requirements) and major deliverables, it is a key input to the quality plan.
- *Product Description.* This elaborates on details and technical issues that could relate to quality.
- *Standards and Regulations as They Apply to the Deliverables.*

- *Descriptions of Process Outputs in Particular Project Team Disciplines* (e.g., engineering process requirements).

Guidelines for Creating a Formal Quality Plan

Instructions: Follow these steps to build a formal quality plan. You may use the check boxes to mark items as completed.

If you are working with a formal or informal advisory group, you might ask some of its members to work through these guidelines with you.

Step 1: Assemble the following documents:

- Your organization's quality policy
- Project scope statement
- Project product description (preliminary deliverables' specifications)
- Standards and regulations
- Descriptions of process outputs in particular project team disciplines

Step 2: Analyze each of the items assembled in Step 1, and distill from each item a list of operational definitions of quality.

- For each item, complete this statement: "According to this item, quality means . . ."
- Compile the items in a list and sort them into related groups.

Step 3: Based on the list created in Step 2, make checklists that the various project team members can use to inspect for quality. (Checklists should be expressed as "Do this . . ." or "Have you done this . . . ?")

☐ Checklists are created.

Step 4: Develop a statement describing how quality management will be implemented on the project. It should describe specific methods of:

- Quality control—examining specific project results to see if they comply with quality standards, and identifying ways to eliminate causes of unsatisfactory performance[43]
- Quality assurance—evaluating overall project performance on a regular basis to provide confidence that the project will satisfy the relevant project quality standards[44]

☐ Statement of quality control and quality assurance is developed.

WHAT A VETERAN PROJECT MANAGER MIGHT DO

A project management professional might do the following:

- Consult the International Organization for Standards (ISO) standards for guidelines related to quality.

- Use his or her professional network to identify subject-matter experts in related fields and then work with these experts to create a formal quality plan.
- Use the *design of experiments technique* to help identify which variables have the most influence on the overall outcome. This involves computing project costs and durations for various combinations of project elements to determine the one that yields the best quality for the lowest resource consumption.[45]

PITFALLS AND CAUTIONS

It's possible to get stuck in "analysis paralysis" when attempting to create a formal quality plan. This is because both defining quality and discussing quality-related issues inevitably touch on deeply held values and beliefs. While the resolution of these issues is of great importance to the organization, it is inappropriate to tackle them as an add-on to a single project. The project's quality plan should grow logically from your organization's established quality policy, or it should be derived from established quality principles held by your profession.

Therefore, we recommend that you do not attempt to create a formal quality plan for your project unless your organization or your profession already has a solid quality policy in place from which this plan may be drawn.

FOR MORE INFORMATION . . .

See PMI's *PMBOK* item 8, Project Quality Management, and item 8.1, Quality Planning.
See PMI's *Quality Management for Projects and Programs* by Lewis Ireland.

OPTIONAL ACTION ITEM: CREATE A FORMAL PROJECT COMMUNICATIONS PLAN

ASSIGNMENT

Develop a project communications plan.

DESIRED OUTPUT

A communications management plan, including:[46]

- Collection structure
- Distribution structure
- Description of information to be disseminated
- Schedules listing when information will be produced
- A method for updating the communications plan

BACKGROUND INFORMATION

As noted in *PMBOK,* "Project communications . . . provide the critical links among people, ideas, and information that are necessary for success."[47] To make sure everyone is prepared to send and receive communications in the appropriate project language, a communications management process must be planned.

Communications planning involves determining the information and communications needs of the stakeholders: who needs what information, when it will be needed, and how it will be provided to them.[48]

In order to plan project communications, you will need information about:[49]

- The project organization and the project stakeholders' responsibilities and relationships
- Disciplines, departments, and specialties involved in the project
- Logistics—which specific individuals will be involved and at what locations
- External information needs—communicating with the press, government agencies, and so forth
- The communications technology available, particularly as it can support fast and efficient communication by methods that all team members can use easily
- Constraints and assumptions—that is, limitations on the communication media or methods

Guidelines for Developing the Project Communications Plan

Instructions: Follow these steps to build your project communications plan. You may use the check boxes to mark items as completed.

If you are working with a formal or informal advisory group, you might ask some of its members to work through these guidelines with you.

Step 1: Assemble the following:

- List of project stakeholders and their roles, responsibilities, and physical locations
- Any descriptions of communication requirements or related assumptions among stakeholders
- Information about external reporting requirements (What do the public, the press, the government, and other outsiders need to know about the project? How will they find out?)
- Information about technology available to support communication on the project (e.g., fax, e-mail, voice mail, messenger, postal service, radio)
- Information about typical project communications methods for the industry or in your organization

Step 2: Answer this question: "What kind of information does each stakeholder need?"

☐ List of information needed by each stakeholder
☐ Typical information needed by stakeholders on similar projects

Step 3: Analyze all stakeholder information needs and answer this question: "What methods and technologies will provide all information needed by stakeholders without wasting resources on providing unneeded information or using inappropriate technology?"

☐ List of appropriate communications methods and technologies

Step 4: Create a project communications plan that includes information about:

☐ Collection structure—How and by whom will project information be gathered, what information will be gathered, and from whom?
☐ Distribution structure—To whom will information flow, and by what methods?
☐ Description of each type of information to be disseminated—What format, content, level of detail, conventions, and definitions will be used?
☐ Schedules listing when each type of information will be produced
☐ A method for updating the communications plan as the project progresses

---

WORKSHEET: Project Communications Planner

Instructions: Look at the chart below. In the "Who" column, list all of the project stakeholders who will need information as the project unfolds. (You may want to list some stakeholders as a group, such as "Engineering" or "Marketing." However, be careful that you have a clear idea about the specific people within the group to whom communications should be going.)

In the "What Information" column, list the type of information this person or group will need.

In the "When" column, list how often or at what points in the project this person or group will need the information. (For example, you might say "weekly" or "monthly" here, or "at sign-off of Phase II.")

In the "How (Form/Medium)" column, list the appropriate medium of communication. (For example, you might say "e-mail status report," "team meeting," "broadcast voice-mail," or "update to project web page.")

Who	What Information	When	How (Form/Medium)

What a Veteran Project Manager Might Do

What a seasoned project manager might do to complete this step is not substantially different from what a novice should do. He or she would simply have more experience creating communications plans and be better able to eliminate inappropriate alternatives quickly.

In addition, a veteran project manager might contact peers in his or her professional network and discuss the pros and cons of different communication techniques.

Pitfalls and Cautions

With so many new technologies available to support communication, it's easy to become mesmerized by fancy bells and whistles. However, there is no substitute for simplicity and discipline.

Consider this example: E-mail is fast and efficient, but sometimes e-mail messages become overblown, needlessly complicated, or so frequent that recipients become numb to them. Or users allow their e-mail boxes to become full because they are "too busy" to download their mail. When these things are allowed to happen, then a powerful technology becomes useless.

The same caution applies to a voice-mail box, a fax machine, or an in-box full of paper. The technology is only as effective as the person using it. All project team members should keep the following in mind when communicating with each other:

- Communicate only as needed.
- Communicate succinctly. Use bulleted lists, and try to make it a rule never to exceed a one-minute verbal message or a single page of text.
- This enforced brevity can make project messages more welcome among team members. What's more, requiring brevity has the added benefit of making people think through their messages before they send them. This can allow time for emotions to cool and encourage senders to conceive of their own solutions to problems.
- Stay on top of your mail, whether e-mail, voice mail, fax, or other form of communication. Read or listen, and then respond within hours, not days.

As project manager, you will set the tone for project communications. By communicating effectively, you will encourage everyone on the team to do likewise.

FOR MORE INFORMATION . . .

See PMI's *PMBOK* item 10, Project Communications Management, and item 10.1, Communications Planning.

ACTION ITEM: ORGANIZE AND ACQUIRE STAFF

Caution: This Action Item describes comprehensive organizational planning and staffing approaches that might be overkill for a smaller project. Use your judgment to determine how many of the elements listed here make sense for your project.

ASSIGNMENT

Develop an organizational plan and a strategy for acquiring staff.

DESIRED OUTPUTS

Desired outputs include:[50]

- Role and responsibility assignments
- Staffing plan
- Organizational chart
- Organization detail as appropriate
- Project staff
- Project team directory

BACKGROUND INFORMATION

Organizational planning involves identifying, documenting, and assigning project roles, responsibilities, and reporting relationships.[51] Acquiring staff involves getting the human resources (individuals or groups) assigned to and working on the project.[52] Most often, organizational planning is done as part of the earliest project phases. However, the organizational plan should be reviewed regularly to ensure it makes sense.[53]

When planning the project organization, these things may be considered:[54]

- Project interfaces
  —Organization Interfaces—reporting relationships among different organizational units (subcontractors, departments, etc.)
  —Technical Interfaces—reporting relationships among different technical disciplines (engineers, builders, etc.)
  —Interpersonal Interfaces—reporting relationships among different individuals
- Staffing requirements. What skills are needed from which individuals or groups in what time frames?
- Constraints
  —Organizational structure
  —Collective bargaining agreements

—Preferences of the project management team
—Expected staff assignments

When staffing the project organization, these things might be considered:[55]

- Staffing Plan—the project staffing requirements as identified during the organizational planning above
- Staffing Pool Description—the previous experiences, personal interests and characteristics, and availability of potential staff members
- Recruitment Practices—policies, guidelines, or procedures that apply to recruitment

Guidelines for Developing the Organizational Plan and Strategy for Acquiring Staff

Instructions: Follow these steps to develop the organizational plan and strategy for acquiring staff. You may use the check boxes to mark items as completed.

If you are working with a formal or informal advisory group, you might ask some of its members to work through these guidelines with you.

Step 1: Given your description of project activities in earlier statements of scope, and so forth, list the job titles (roles) of people who will be needed to complete each activity.

- Job titles or roles are listed.

Step 2: For each job title, list the responsibilities (tasks) to be performed. Consult these sources as needed:

- Project templates—role and responsibility definitions from similar projects
- Organization-specific human resource practices—policies, guidelines, and procedures that dictate how people are deployed (e.g., Will managers serve as coaches? If so, then what exactly is the role of coach?)
- Organizational theory—texts related to human resource management and the structure of project teams

☐ Job responsibilities are listed.

Step 3: Create a Responsibility/Accountability Matrix—for example:[56]

RESPONSIBILITY/ACCOUNTABILITY MATRIX					
Phase ↘ *Person* →	Bill	Charmaine	Juan	Leticia	Mary
Determine Need and Feasibility	A	S	P	P	P

Create the Project Plan	A	S, I	I	I	I
Create Deliverables' Specifications	A, P	S	R	P	P
Create Deliverables	A, 4	S	P	P	P
Test and Implement	A	I	R	R	P
P = Participate, A = Accountable, R = Review, I = Input Required, S = Sign-off Required					

☐ Responsibility/Accountability Matrix is created.

Step 4: Create a staffing plan that answers these questions:[57]

- When and how will people be added?
- Will the project use both internal and external resources? (Refer to Optional Action Item: Plan for and Acquire Outside Resources.)
- When will people be let go from the project team?
- How long should people be held when there is downtime (absence of work on their assigned activity)?

☐ Staffing plan is created.

Step 5: Create an organization chart that graphically displays project reporting relationships.[58] The chart should take into account reporting relationships among:

- Different organizational units (subcontractors, departments, etc.)
- Different technical disciplines (engineers, builders, etc.)
- Different individuals

☐ Organization chart is created.

Step 6: Flesh out the organizational plan with these details as needed:

- Warnings describing what you will not be able to do if you cannot staff the project as recommended. (Describe what project deliverables cannot be created, how the schedule will be delayed, how safety may be jeopardized, and so on.)
- Specific job descriptions or position descriptions, including job title, skills, responsibilities, knowledge, authority, expected physical work environment, and so on.
- Training needs, if the staff to be acquired may not have all the skills required.

☐ Warnings related to essential staffing are stated.
☐ Job descriptions and training needs are detailed.

Step 7: Use appropriate procurement practices to identify and recruit resources. Take into account the staffing plan from Step 4, as well as standard recruiting practices dictated by your organization's policies (also see Optional Action Item: Plan for and Acquire Outside Resources).

- Identify resources.
- Recruit resources.
- Confirm resources as part of project team.

Step 8: When all (or most) staff positions have been filled, create a project team directory consisting of:

- Names of team members and stakeholders
- How to reach each person listed (fax, phone, e-mail, postal service address, and so on)
- Other information such as direct reports, responsibilities, administrative support people, and so on as needed

☐ Project team directory is created.

WORKSHEET: Project Responsibility/Accountability Matrix

Instructions: Using this matrix, list the project phases, activities, or deliverables in the first column. Label each of the remaining columns with the name of a project team member. Fill in the blanks underneath each team member's name with the appropriate initial to indicate his or her role related to this phase, activity, or deliverable. (Example: "I" for input, "S" for sign-off.) Try to avoid using more than one initial per cell on the grid.

Note: For best results, consider making this a team effort and complete the worksheet early in the project.

PROJECT RESPONSIBILITY/ACCOUNTABILITY MATRIX						
Phase* ↓	Person →					

P = Participate A = Accountable R = Review I = Input Required S = Sign-off Required

This column might also be labeled "activities" or "deliverables."

What a Veteran Project Manager Might Do

What a project management professional might do to complete this step is not substantially different from what a novice should do. He or she would simply have more experience and templates available, and thus would be better able to perform some of the action items quickly.

In addition, veteran project managers typically have a pool of experienced people from whom they prefer to draw to get quality results, or they have a network of peers with whom they can discuss various staffing strategies or from whom they can obtain recommendations regarding the strengths and weaknesses of individual resources.

Pitfalls and Cautions

Take nothing for granted! It's easy for the novice to make all sorts of assumptions. Some of these include:

- Assuming you and the interviewee (potential team member) have exactly the same picture of what his or her responsibilities will be
- Assuming you are not violating government or organizational recruiting practices
- Assuming you know the exact legal relationship of the team member to the team (Is the recruit legally regarded as a contractor? An employee? Part time? Full time? And what does this status mean in terms of paperwork and your management practices?)
- Assuming all the stakeholders will find the person recruited to be acceptable

The bottom line: Probe and do your homework to make sure you and the person recruited fully understand all the aspects of the job, the legal relationship you are establishing, the person's exact place in your organization, and the stakeholders' likely approval, to name just a few necessities.

In short, assume nothing! Spell it out, check it off, and get it in writing.

Caution: When you are acquiring human resources from other organizations, keep in mind that sometimes functional department heads may try to keep their best people for themselves, instead donating a rookie or weaker performer to your project. Or a functional department head may try to call back a person from your project team by rearranging his or her priorities after your project has begun. For these reasons, we recommend that you specify in writing exactly what the skill level of the resource should be and obtain a written, contractual commitment that the resource will be yours for the duration of your project. At minimum, ensure that you and the functional department heads exchange memos outlining each party's expectations regarding shared resources.

For More Information . . .

House, Ruth Sizemore. *The Human Side of Project Management.* Reading, MA: Addison-Wesley, 1988.

Nelson, Bob, and Economy, Peter. *Managing for Dummies,* Foster City, CA: IDG Books, 1996.

Pell, Arthur. *Complete Idiot's Guide to Managing People.* New York: Alpha Books, 1995.

See PMI's *PMBOK* item 9, Project Human Resource Management; item 9.1, Organizational Planning; and item 9.2, Staff Acquisition.

See PMI's *Roles and Responsibilities of the Project Manager* by John Adams and Bryan Campbell.

See PMI's *Organizing for Project Management* by Dwayne Cable and John Adams.

See PMI's *Team Building for Project Managers* by Linn Stuckenbruck and David Marshall.

See PMI's *Conflict Management for Project Managers* by Nicki Kirchof and John Adams.

In addition, there is a vast body of literature describing how to deal with people in an ongoing, operational context. The topics that may be of interest include organizational structures, leadership, conflict resolution, delegating, team building, recruitment, and labor relations. You might start by asking your peers for their favorite texts on related topics or by consulting the catalog of a reputable publisher in the field.

See also Appendix A: Tips for Managing Experts Outside Your Expertise at the end of this book.

OPTIONAL ACTION ITEM: IDENTIFY RISKS AND PLAN TO RESPOND

ASSIGNMENT

Given a potential project, identify risks and plan to respond to them.

DESIRED OUTPUT

A document that describes the following:[59]

- Sources of risk
- Potential risk events
- Risk symptoms
- Ways to improve other processes or activities
- Opportunities to pursue or threats to which to respond
- Opportunities or threats to ignore
- Risk management plan
- Contingency plans
- Descriptions of desired reserves
- Contractual agreements to mitigate risks

BACKGROUND INFORMATION

The term *risk* is commonly used with two different meanings: it can mean uncertainty, or it can mean threat. We use the term here to mean uncertainty. Furthermore, the processes described here are sometimes referred to as risk analysis, risk assessment, response planning, risk mitigation, or risk management.[60]

PMBOK provides these definitions:

- "Risk identification consists of determining what sources of risk and which risk events may be reasonably expected to affect the project." Risk identification is an ongoing process, not a one-time task, and should be conducted regularly throughout the project.[61]
- "Risk quantification is primarily concerned with determining which risk events warrant response."[62]

A number of factors complicate the process of quantifying risks. As *PMBOK* notes:

- "Opportunities and threats can interact in unanticipated ways (schedule delays may force . . . a new strategy which could reduce overall project duration)."
- "A single risk event could cause multiple effects (late delivery of a key compo-

nent could lead to cost overruns, schedule delays, penalty payments, and a lower-quality product).''

- ''Opportunities for one stakeholder (reduced costs) may be threats to another (reduced profits).''
- ''The mathematical techniques to quantify risk can create a false sense of precision or reliability.''[63]

Developing a risk response is the process of deciding what to do to address a risk. There are several choices:[64]

- Avoid it by eliminating the cause.
- Mitigate it by reducing the expected monetary value.
- Accept it and take the consequences.

Guidelines for Identifying Risks and Planning to Respond

Instructions: Follow these steps to identify project risks and to plan responses to them. You may use the check boxes to mark items as completed.

If you are working with a formal or informal advisory group, you might ask its members to work through these guidelines with you.

Step 1: Determine what sources of risk and which risk events may reasonably be expected to affect the project.[65]

- Examine the product (deliverables) description. Which require creation by using unproven technology? Or which deliverables are themselves made up of unproven technology?
- Examine the scope statement. Are the project costs or objectives overly aggressive?
- Examine the work breakdown structure. Are there hidden dependencies that should be explored? Could the work breakdown structure be broken into greater detail in some areas to shine a light on risks or opportunities? If so, then create this detail.
- Examine the staffing plan. Are there ''irreplaceable'' team members who might be made unavailable somehow?
- Examine the resource requirements (people, equipment, and materials). Could market conditions make it difficult to obtain some resources (a risk) or easier to obtain some resources (an opportunity)?
- Examine the history of similar projects. What potential opportunities or threats might you identify based on previous experience?
- Use established checklists from your project's discipline to evaluate risk and opportunities.
- Interview various stakeholders to uncover opportunities or risks.

Step 2: Quantify the risks identified in Step 1 to determine which risk events warrant response. Consider:

- Expected monetary value or impact of the risk
- Expected impact on project quality
- Expected impact on project schedule

☐ Risks are quantified.

Step 3: Decide which risks or opportunities to focus on and document them by making a list of "risks to pursue."

☐ "Risks to Pursue" list is created.

Step 4: For each risk warranting response, choose one of these risk responses:[66]

- Avoid it by eliminating the cause.

    This might involve using different approaches to the work process, different staffing, redefined deliverables, revised (lower-risk) schedules, or modified stakeholder expectations.

- Mitigate it by reducing the expected monetary value. For example, you could:
    —Contract out high-risk activities to specialists who have more experience.
    —Obtain insurance policies to deal with some types of risk.
    —Develop contingency plans that identify specific actions to take if an identified risk should occur.
    —Set aside a desired reserve of cash or other resources to use if the risk occurs.
- Accept it and take the consequences.

For help with this analysis, see Worksheet: Risk Assessment and Response Analyzer.

☐ Each risk is examined, and a decision to avoid, mitigate, or accept it is made.

Step 5: Create a risk management plan that contains these sections:

- List of potential risk events
- Description of risk symptoms
- Ways to improve processes or activities to reduce risks
- Opportunities to pursue or threats to which to respond
- Opportunities or threats that have been identified and consciously ignored
- Description of contingency plans and steps to take to mitigate risks
- Recommended contractual agreements to mitigate risks

☐ Risk management plan is created.

WORKSHEET: Risk Assessment and Response Analyzer

Instructions: Make a list of risks to your project. Using the grid, examine each risk separately, and try to place it in the appropriate grid cell. Using the hints provided in each cell, determine an appropriate response to the risk.

For example, let's say that we are managing a technical project that faces the risk of losing the only scientist who understands the science behind the project. This would be enormously damaging to the project. At the same time, we know that she is being aggressively pursued by other companies and is unhappy with her current salary. This means it is highly likely that she will leave before the project is completed. Given these circumstances, this risk fits into the upper-right grid square (high potential damage, high likelihood). So our overall approach should be to avoid this risk by eliminating its cause. We may do this by obtaining a higher salary for her, by hiring someone else with equivalent expertise as a backup, or by insisting that she thoroughly train others so they develop her level of expertise.

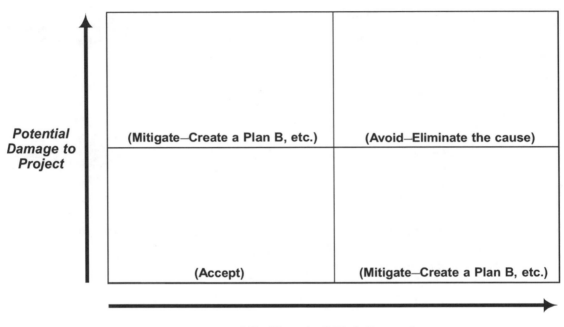

Likelihood of Risk Occurring

WHAT A VETERAN PROJECT MANAGER MIGHT DO

A veteran project manager is likely to contact members of his or her network to discuss their experiences with risks encountered on similar projects and the ways to mitigate them.

A project management professional might engage in all sorts of sophisticated analyses to come up with numbers to quantify the risks. These analyses might include:[67]

- Calculating expected monetary values of risks by multiplying risk event probability by risk event value
- Summing probability distributions of cost estimates, quantity estimates, and similar items
- Conducting schedule simulations to provide statistical distributions of the likelihood of achieving particular project results

■ Employing decision trees to depict complex interactions among decisions and associated chance events

PITFALLS AND CAUTIONS

It is easier to ignore risks than to address them formally. In fact, formal risk planning is unusual. It's not often done on projects.

However, we recommend that you at least review the guideline items and consider them for the types of projects you typically encounter in your industry. Then decide whether you should create a formal risk management plan.

FOR MORE INFORMATION . . .

See PMI's *PMBOK* item 11, item 11.1, item 11.2, and item 11.3.

See PMI's *Project and Program Risk Management: A Guide to Managing Project Risks and Opportunities,* edited by R. Max Wideman.

OPTIONAL ACTION ITEM: PLAN FOR AND ACQUIRE OUTSIDE RESOURCES

ASSIGNMENT

Describe your strategy for procuring outside goods or services, soliciting bids, and selecting the best contractor for the job.

DESIRED OUTPUT

A procurement management plan indicating the following:[68]

- Types of contracts to be used among contractors or vendors
- How estimates from vendors will be obtained
- Responsibilities of the project management team versus people in any procurement department
- How to use any standardized procurement documents
- Statement of work (SOW) or statement of requirements (SOR) describing the item (product or service) to be procured. The statement should provide prospective contractors with enough detail that they can evaluate their ability to provide the item.
- Bid documents, such as RFP (request for proposal), IFB (invitation for bid), invitation for quotation, and similar documents
- Evaluation criteria—means of scoring contractors' proposals to select the most appropriate for the job
- Contract with one or more suppliers of goods or services

BACKGROUND INFORMATION

Procurement means acquiring goods and services from outside the immediate project organization. Depending on the industry, the seller of goods and services may be called a contractor, supplier, or vendor. One of these terms may have negative connotations in one industry but not in another.[69]

The company that acts as seller (contractor, supplier, or vendor) will typically manage the creation of its own work product (the goods or services to be delivered). In this case, the buyer becomes a customer of the seller, and thus is a key stakeholder in the seller's project. However, the seller's project management team must be concerned with the processes used to manage the larger project to which they are contributing, not just those required to provide their goods or services. Thus, the project manager of the larger project must clearly communicate the parameters of the seller's role in the larger project. Not surprisingly, the terms and conditions of the seller's contract become a key input to many project management processes. This is because the contract may describe its own milestones, cost objectives, staffing limitations, and so on. All of these must be rolled up into the overall project plan.[70]

Procurement planning is the process of identifying which project needs can be best met by procuring goods or services outside the internal project team.[71] Since the overall project's sponsor is likely to have a desire to control certain crucial project elements, any contracts with outside suppliers must conform to sponsor expectations as well as to project manager expectations.

Procurement planning results in a decision to do one of these things:[72]

- Procure all or virtually all goods and services through a single, prime contractor
- Procure a significant portion of the goods and services required from multiple contractors
- Procure a minor portion of the goods and services required from contractors
- Procure nothing from contractors

Solicitation planning (planning to solicit bids from contractors) involves preparing all the documents needed to support solicitation of bids.[73]

Solicitation involves obtaining bids and proposals from prospective contractors about how they may meet project needs.[74] Most of the effort in this process is expended by prospective contractors, who normally prepare their bids at no cost to the project.

Source selection (choosing a contractor) involves receiving bids or proposals from prospective contractors and applying evaluation criteria to select the best one for the job.[75]

Guidelines for Planning to Procure Outside Goods or Services

Instructions: Follow these steps to plan to procure (acquire) the help of outside contractors to provide certain goods or services for your project. You may use the check boxes to mark items as completed.

If you are working with a formal or informal advisory group, you might ask some of its members to work through these guidelines with you.

Step 1: Assemble the following:

- Scope statement
- Detailed product description (details of all deliverables to be created)
- Description of resources that support procurement (procurement department, internal project experts who can help find contractors, professional directories, and so on)
- Information on market conditions for the particular type of contractor you are trying to procure
- Any relevant planning inputs, such as cost estimates and quality management plans
- Constraints and assumptions that will likely limit options (such as funds or schedule)

Step 2: Decide to make or buy the goods or services.

- Examine the costs and benefits of creating the goods or services yourself. Consider:
  - Workload of existing resources
  - The time required to locate and acquire additional resources (such as new staff or new equipment)
  - Your expertise in managing these resources
  - Whether you want to have this resource available on an ongoing basis, as part of your organization
- Examine the costs and benefits of procuring the goods or services from an outside contractor. Consider:
  - The actual cost of purchase compared to the cost of using internal resources
  - The cost (including headaches and time spent) in soliciting bids and selecting vendors
  - What external contractors can provide that your organization cannot or should not be able to provide on an ongoing basis
- Involve subject-matter experts from the project team, industry groups, consultant organizations, or even prospective contractors in these preliminary discussions.
- Decide to buy goods or services from an outside resource.

   Note: If you decide to make the goods or perform the services internally, stop here.

Step 3: Create a procurement management plan indicating the following:[76]

- Types of contracts to be used among contractors or vendors
- How estimates from vendors will be obtained
- Responsibilities of the project management team versus responsibilities of people in any procurement department
- How to use any standardized procurement documents

☐ Procurement management plan is created.

Step 4: Create a statement of work (SOW) or statement of requirements (SOR) describing the item (product, deliverables, or service) to be procured. The statement should provide prospective contractors with enough detail that they can evaluate their ability to provide the item.[77]

☐ Statement of work or requirements is created.

Step 5: Create bid documents, such as RFP (request for proposal), IFB (invitation for bid), invitation for quotation, and similar documents.[78]

- Refer to any standard forms required by your organization.
- Refer to past versions of these documents for similar projects, and use boilerplate text if appropriate.
- Discuss your draft bid documents with someone who has solicited bids similar to yours.

☐ RFP, IFP, or similar document are finalized.

Step 6: Create bid or proposal evaluation criteria (means of scoring contractors' proposals). Consider these typical criteria and possibly weight some of them to count higher than others:

- Cost
- Quality
- Vendor team members
- Track record
- Facilities and equipment
- Creativity of proposal
- Referrals from former customers
- Ability to meet the schedule

☐ Bid or proposal evaluation criteria are established.

Guidelines for Soliciting Bids for Outside Goods or Services

Instructions: Follow these steps to solicit bids or proposals from outside contractors to provide certain goods or services for your project. You may use the check boxes to mark items as completed.

If you are working with a formal or informal advisory group, you might ask some of its members to work through these guidelines with you.

Step 1: Identify potential suppliers by asking for peer recommendations (people in professional groups, competitor organizations, others in your organization who know good potential vendors) or by examining listings of suppliers in directories of professional organizations, and so on.

- Potential suppliers are identified.

Step 2: Decide whether to send out bid documents, advertise in professional journals or newspapers, or conduct a bidders' conference to solicit bids.

- Decide how to disseminate requests for bids.

Step 3: Send out bid documents, conduct the bidders' information session, and/or place advertisements.

- Send out bid documents.

Step 4: Clarify questions from potential contractors as needed.

- Clarify contractor questions.

Step 5: Accept bids or proposals as they arrive, and disseminate them to fellow decision makers as appropriate.

- Accept and disseminate bids or proposals among decision makers.

Guidelines for Selecting the Best Contractor for the Job

Instructions: Follow these steps to choose the best contractor from several who have submitted bids or proposals to provide certain goods or services for your project. You may use the check boxes to mark items as completed.

If you are working with a formal or informal advisory group, you might ask some of its members to work through these guidelines with you.

Step 1: Review your bid or proposal evaluation criteria (means of scoring contractors' proposals) (see Step 6 of Worksheet: Guidelines for Planning to Procure Outside Goods or Services).

- Evaluation criteria are reviewed.

Step 2: Set up a bid or proposal scoring sheet, which might include a weighting system (numerical weight assigned to each criterion) and a statement of minimum requirements (e.g., "Bid must be under $50,000 and maintain a schedule of no longer than 4 months").

Here is an example of such a scoring sheet:

Criteria	Possible Score	Jones Corp.	Smith Corp.	XYZ Corp.
Cost	6	4	6	6
Track record	8	8	5	5
Team members	10	10	10	5
Creativity	10	7	10	10
(. . . and so on)	. . .	. . .	. . .	. . .
Total score	50	40	35	45

☐ Scoring sheet is created.

Step 3: If appropriate, screen each bid or proposal and eliminate some on the basis of failing to meet the minimum requirements.

☐ Preliminary cut is completed, eliminating some contractors.

Step 4: Review all qualifying proposals and apply scoring criteria. If appropriate, ask a peer to cross-check your evaluations. (This person should be an experienced buyer of outside services who can help you cut through the puffery typically found in contractor proposals. It would be even more valuable if this person has direct experience working with one or more of the bidders.)

☐ Bids or proposals are scored.

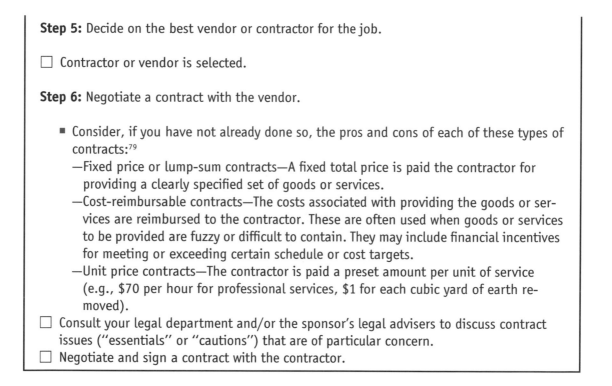

Step 5: Decide on the best vendor or contractor for the job.

☐ Contractor or vendor is selected.

Step 6: Negotiate a contract with the vendor.

- Consider, if you have not already done so, the pros and cons of each of these types of contracts:[79]
  —Fixed price or lump-sum contracts—A fixed total price is paid the contractor for providing a clearly specified set of goods or services.
  —Cost-reimbursable contracts—The costs associated with providing the goods or services are reimbursed to the contractor. These are often used when goods or services to be provided are fuzzy or difficult to contain. They may include financial incentives for meeting or exceeding certain schedule or cost targets.
  —Unit price contracts—The contractor is paid a preset amount per unit of service (e.g., $70 per hour for professional services, $1 for each cubic yard of earth removed).
☐ Consult your legal department and/or the sponsor's legal advisers to discuss contract issues ("essentials" or "cautions") that are of particular concern.
☐ Negotiate and sign a contract with the contractor.

WHAT A VETERAN PROJECT MANAGER MIGHT DO

What a veteran project manager might do to complete this step is not substantially different from what a novice should do. He or she would simply have more experience creating bids, selecting vendors, and negotiating contracts.

In addition, the experienced veteran is likely to have relationships with many potential contractors in his or her industry and be familiar with their strengths and weaknesses.

Finally, a veteran project manager is likely to contact members of his or her network of peers inside and outside the organization to discuss issues associated with finding, selecting, justifying, and handling the paperwork for outside resources.

PITFALLS AND CAUTIONS

Outside procurement can be a difficult and time-consuming process. Plan on spending plenty of time (probably more than you imagine) on all of the Action Items.

Caution: The novice project manager should *not* undertake these activities without the help of a more experienced person. In working with outside resources, there is the potential for legal snarls, financial difficulties, and disagreements over the quality of their work processes or deliverables. If you have never procured outside resources, you should get help from a supervisor, a peer, a professional contact at another company who has worked with outside resources, or anyone else who has been through the process for a project similar to the one you are planning.

For More Information . . .

See PMI's *PMBOK* item 12, Project Procurement Management; item 12.1, Procurement Planning; item 12.2, Solicitation Planning; item 12.3, Solicitation; and item 12.4, Source Selection.

See PMI's *Negotiating and Contracting for Project Management* by Penny Cavendish and Martin D. Martin.

See PMI's *Contract Administration for the Project Manager* by Martin D. Martin, C. Claude Teagarden, and Charles F. Lambreth.

ACTION ITEM: ORGANIZE THE PROJECT PLAN

ASSIGNMENT

Create a comprehensive project plan.

DESIRED OUTPUT

A comprehensive project plan that pulls together all the outputs of the preceding project planning activities. For a detailed description of the project plan components, see Guidelines for Building the Project Plan.

BACKGROUND INFORMATION

The project plan is a formal, approved document used to guide both project execution and project control. The project plan is based on the outputs of other planning processes. The project plan is almost always revised several times through preliminary drafts, reviews, and revisions.

   PMBOK notes that the project plan is used to do the following:

- Guide project execution
- Document project planning assumptions
- Document project planning decisions regarding alternatives chosen
- Facilitate communication among stakeholders
- Define key management reviews as to content, extent, and timing
- Provide a baseline for measuring project progress and for project control[80]

Guidelines for Building the Project Plan

Instructions: Follow these steps to develop a formal, written plan for your project. You may use the check boxes to mark items as completed.

   If you are working with a formal or informal advisory group, you might ask some of its members to work through these guidelines with you.

Step 1: Assemble all the outputs of the preceding action items (i.e., scope statement, cost estimates, schedules, quality plan, etc.).
☐ Outputs of preceding planning Action Items are assembled.

Step 2: Develop an outline or table of contents for your project plan. It might include any of the following, as appropriate for your project:[81]
   - Project charter—document issued by senior management that provides the project manager with the authority to apply organizational resources to project activities

---

- Scope statement—description of the sum of the products and services to be provided by the project
- Work breakdown structure (WBS) to a level of detail that will be used to execute the project
- Cost estimates, scheduled start dates, and responsibility assignments to the level of the WBS at which control will be exercised
- Progress measurement baselines for time and cost
- Major milestones
- Detailed project schedules
- Key or required staff
- Key risks (including constraints and assumptions) and planned response for each
- Open issues and pending decisions
- Other information as needed for the particular project
- Appendixes or supporting documents with detailed information such as technical documentation, preliminary specifications and preliminary designs

Step 3: Review your outline with the sponsor and key stakeholders. Obtain their feedback regarding enhancements.

☐ Project plan outline is reviewed with stakeholders.

Step 4: Revise your outline based on results of Step 3.

☐ Outline is revised.

Step 5: Write the project plan by knitting together the pieces you assembled in Step 1.

- Write an overall introduction to the plan.
- Write transitions to help the reader comprehend the connections (inevitable linkages) among parts of the plan.
- Write an executive summary summarizing and highlighting the contents of the plan.
- Circulate a draft of the plan for review.
- Obtain feedback and revise and recirculate as needed.

☐ Project plan is written.

Step 6: Circulate the final project plan among sponsor or customer and key stakeholders.

☐ Project plan is circulated among sponsor or customer and key stakeholders.

WHAT A VETERAN PROJECT MANAGER MIGHT DO

What a seasoned project manager might do to complete this step is not substantially different from what a novice should do. He or she would simply have more experience assembling the pieces, have more models (examples) available, and have more experience working with sponsors and stakeholders to develop the plan.

PITFALLS AND CAUTIONS

Novice project managers might be tempted to spend lots of time polishing and re-working the plan before allowing stakeholders to see it. *However, we recommend that stakeholders be involved early and often in the process of building the plan,* when it is rough and malleable—and when the project manager is less ego involved in every word. In this way, stakeholders will know they are being asked to make meaningful contributions, since it will be obvious that the plan is a work in progress. In addition, having everyone participate in the plan's creation can help build bonds early among team members and help ensure that the plan is supported by all stakeholders.

FOR MORE INFORMATION . . .

See PMI's *PMBOK* item 4.1, Project Plan Development.

Action Item: Close Out the Project Planning Phase

Assignment

Close out the project planning phase.

Desired Outputs

- A project plan that has been approved by sponsor or customer and key stakeholders
- Documentation (written and signed documents) that indicates the sponsor:
  —Approves the project plan.
  —Provides a green light or okay to begin work on the project.

Background Information

After the project plan has been reviewed by sponsors and key stakeholders, it is time to obtain formal commitment and approval to begin the project.

Because the execution of the project will typically require substantial organizational resources (people, equipment, materials, and money), formal approval is essential. The project planning phase is closed out by obtaining this formal approval.

Guidelines for Closing Out the Project Planning Phase

Instructions: Follow these steps to plan to close out the project planning phase for your project. You may use the check boxes to mark items as completed.

If you are working with a formal or informal advisory group, you might ask some of its members to work through these guidelines with you.

Step 1: If you have not already done so, circulate the formal project plan among reviewers, including sponsor and key stakeholders.

☐ Project plan is circulated.

Step 2: Conduct a formal, face-to-face meeting with the sponsor and key stakeholders in which you do the following:

- Briefly walk through the project plan, highlighting important sections.
- Discuss each of the sections until all attendees are comfortable with the plan.

  Caution: Be certain to face up to the most controversial parts of the plan and discuss them at length. Do not avoid them or gloss over them, since they may come back to haunt you later and you may need considerable sponsor support to overcome associated difficulties.

- Obtain concurrence among attendees about the plan, and if appropriate, decide on a strategy for modifying the plan.
- Present the sponsor with a sign-off document that indicates his or her approval of the entire project plan, with annotations listing needed changes. (See the sample in Action Item: Close Out Project Activities.)

☐ Obtain the sponsor signature on the sign-off document.

> *Note:* If you cannot obtain sponsor approval of the plan, decide which sections need to be modified and agree on a strategy for making modifications and a deadline for completing them. Repeat Steps 1 and 2 if needed.

Step 3: After you have obtained formal approval of the project plan, summarize the results of the meeting and send out to other parts of the organization a formal announcement providing a thumbnail description of the project.

> *Caution:* Do not begin the project without formal, public approval of the project plan from the sponsor. To do so would mean you are taking responsibility for expending the organization's resources without authority or sponsor support.

What a Veteran Project Manager Might Do

What a project management professional might do to complete this step is not substantially different from what a novice should do. He or she would simply have more experience working with sponsors and other stakeholders to obtain consensus.

One technique that a veteran project manager might use is to hold several mini-meetings or brief phone discussions with each of the sponsors or stakeholders before conducting any formal approval meetings. In this way, the manager would be able to address specific issues one-on-one with each individual. This can prevent surprises or blow-ups when the formal plan approval meeting is held.

Generally, a project management professional is more likely to tackle head-on the tough and controversial issues associated with the project, because he or she knows that such issues can come back to bite you later if glossed over at the beginning of the project.

Pitfalls and Cautions

A novice project manager, eager to get the project started, may be tempted to sidestep or even ignore difficult or controversial issues in order to get the project plan approved and get things moving. However, this is extremely dangerous, since what in the planning phase is a small dissatisfaction on the part of a stakeholder can grow into larger frustrations as the project unfolds. In the worst cases, frustrated stakeholders have been known to drag their feet on key project reviews, refuse to approve deliverables or provide essential input, and cause all sorts of problems on the project.

We recommend that when closing out your project plan, you encourage a frank discussion of even the most minor concerns identified by stakeholders. Give stakeholders time to process these issues, airing their grievances and identifying corresponding changes in the plan. Then develop a true consensus, seeking to incorporate responses to all the issues they identified. If your project is like most others, you will need the wholehearted support of the entire team to make it a success.

FOR MORE INFORMATION . . .

See PMI's *PMBOK* item 5.4, Scope Verification, and item 10.4, Administrative Closure.

ACTION ITEM: REVISIT THE PROJECT PLAN AND REPLAN IF NEEDED

ASSIGNMENT

Review the approved project plan at the beginning of each project phase to ensure the plan is still accurate.

DESIRED OUTPUT

Confidence on the part of the project manager that the detailed plans to execute a particular phase are still accurate and will effectively achieve results as planned

BACKGROUND INFORMATION

The detailed project plan should account for all the activities associated with each particular phase. However, it is often the case that considerable time passes between the conclusion of one phase and the beginning of the next. Passage of time can result in many changes, including:

- Changes in stakeholders
- Changes in availability of resources
- Changes in sponsor's strategic direction
- Changes in funding
- Changes in external forces (environmental, economic, etc.) that influence the project

Therefore, if substantial time has passed since the initial project plan was approved, it is prudent for the project manager to revisit the project plan at the beginning of each phase to make sure that it remains accurate for that phase.

Guidelines for Revisiting the Plan and Replanning if Needed

Instructions: Follow these steps to confirm that the project plan remains accurate for a particular project phase. You may use the check boxes to mark items as completed.

Step 1: Locate the detailed project plan, as approved at the end of Phase II: Create Project Plan.

☐ The detailed project plan is located.

Step 2: Examine all project plans as they relate to this particular phase.

☐ All project plans are examined.

Step 3: Evaluate the plans by considering these questions:

Yes	No	
❑	❑	Is the scope for this phase still accurate?
❑	❑	Is the project budget still accurate?
❑	❑	Is the project staffing plan still accurate?
❑	❑	Is the list of the project's sponsor and key stakeholders still accurate?

If "yes" to all of these questions, then continue to Step 4.

If "no" to any question, then immediately contact the sponsor to decide whether it is necessary to repeat some or all of the action items described in Phase II: Create Project Plan.

Step 4: When you are satisfied you have an accurate project plan, then you may begin this particular project phase.

❑ Plan is accurate. It's okay to begin this project phase.

WHAT A VETERAN PROJECT MANAGER MIGHT DO

What a project management professional might do to complete this step is not substantially different from what a novice should do. He or she would simply have more experience finding and anticipating ways in which circumstances have changed since the initial plan was created.

PITFALLS AND CAUTIONS

It's tempting to simply begin a project phase without going back to the detailed project plan and confirming the accuracy of the scope, budget, staffing plan, and so on. This is risky, since there is a chance that the scope or other project elements have changed as a result of executing the preceding phase or because of changes in the organization funding the project, changes in the marketplace, and so on.

We recommend that you briefly revisit the project plan at the beginning of every phase and confirm the continued relevance of the plan with the sponsor and stakeholders. This will help ensure that you either:

- Build the deliverables as promised in the plan
- Understand how the scope (deliverables, resources required, etc.) must change so that you may adjust the stakeholders' expectations before you execute the changes

EXECUTING

Executing is the process by which project plans are carried out. Executing involves these activities:

- Project plan execution
- Team development
- Information distribution
- Solicitation and source selection
- Contract administration

For more details, see the expanded description of this process in Part II: Your Essential Project Actions.

The following Action Item supports the process of executing:

- Action Item: Execute Project Activities

ACTION ITEM: EXECUTE PROJECT ACTIVITIES

ASSIGNMENT

Execute a particular project activity or phase as planned.

DESIRED OUTPUTS

- Work results (deliverables associated with this activity or phase) are created as a result of executing the project activities.[82]
- Change requests (i.e., changes resulting in expanded or contracted project scope related to deliverables specifications) are identified.[83]
- Periodic progress reports summarizing results of activities are created.[84]
- Team performance is assessed, guided, and improved if needed through training and other interventions (e.g., team building, reward and recognition).[85]
- Bids or proposals for deliverables associated with this phase are solicited, contractors (suppliers) are chosen, and contracts are established.[86]
- Contracts are administered to achieve desired work results (communication with contractors is undertaken to obtain work as planned, contract changes are prepared and negotiated as needed, contractors are paid).[87]

BACKGROUND INFORMATION

It is difficult to provide generic background information about how to execute specific project activities or phases. At this point, the particular professionals working in a particular industry set to work executing the activities for which they have been trained. So on a construction project, engineers create blueprints, carpenters build framing, and so on. Or on a motion picture project, scriptwriters write the script, casting people locate talent, directors begin shooting scenes, and so on. In short, people do their assigned jobs to accomplish the project goals.

In order to execute any phase of a project, the project manager must see to it that the project plan is carried out by performing the activities as described in the plan. In particular, this means the project manager should do the following:

- Direct team members to complete activities for which they are responsible.
- Create or supervise other team members in creating progress reports summarizing the results of activities.
- Formally or informally evaluate team performance and decide whether training or other interventions are needed to achieve desired results.
- If appropriate, solicit contractor support; then select the contractor and manage the contractor's work.

Guidelines for Executing a Project Phase

Instructions: Follow these steps to execute a particular project phase or activity. You may use the check boxes to mark items as completed.

Step 1: Review the project plan carefully, and get a clear picture of what the results of this phase should be.

☐ Project plan is reviewed.

Step 2: If appropriate, conduct a kickoff meeting to get the phase off to a good start. The kickoff meeting should accomplish these objectives:

- Clarify the work product (deliverables).
- Clarify the roles and responsibilities of team members.
- Create a shared sense of purpose among team members.
- Obtain the specific commitment of each team member to complete assigned activities according to schedule and budget constraints.
- Make sure all team members have what is needed to begin work on this phase.

   Note: Small projects will likely have only one kickoff meeting, scheduled immediately after approval of the formal plan is obtained. Large, complex, or long-duration projects might require kickoff meetings at the beginning of each project phase.

☐ Kickoff meeting is planned.
☐ Kickoff meeting is conducted.

Step 3: As needed, provide oral or written authorization to project team members to begin work on their activities at the appropriate times.

☐ Team members are authorized to begin.

Step 4: Set up and conduct status review meetings and routine status reporting procedures.

Caution: Make sure meetings are truly justified and waste no team member's time. Consider conference calls or other nontravel options for geographically distant team members.

☐ Status reporting procedures are established.
☐ Status reports are obtained.

Step 5: Based on team performance, provide training and other interventions (team building, reward and recognition, etc.).

☐ Needed team training, reward, and recognition are identified.
☐ Team training, reward, and recognition are provided.

Step 6: Circulate reports of progress according to the project's communications plan. Report progress of deliverables in terms of schedule, cost, and quality considerations. (For a sample status report see Worksheet: The Project Status Report under Action Item: Control Project Activities.)

☐ Progress reports are circulated.

Repeat Steps 3 through 6 as needed.

Guidelines for Recognizing Project Team Members

By definition, project execution involves team development—in particular, assessing and guiding team performance, as well as providing rewards and recognition. In their book *Managing for Dummies,* Bob Nelson and Peter Economy identify ten ways that managers can provide recognition for employees. Below, we've adapted this list for use by project managers. As you work with your team members during project execution, see how many of these methods you can apply.

- *Provide interesting work.* To the extent possible, give project team members the opportunity to go beyond the mundane or the repetitive and become involved in activities that might challenge or fascinate.
- *Provide visibility.* Shine a light on team member contributions; let the world know what they are contributing to the project and how the project is contributing to the overall enterprise's goals. Publishing articles in the company newsletter, posting an announcement on a bulletin board or intranet site, or simply praising a team member's contributions in the presence of his or her supervisors or peers are examples of simple ways project managers can provide visibility for team members.
- *Provide time off.* When project team members have gone the extra mile, working evenings and weekends, recognize the contribution by providing them with time off. Or when there is a lull in project activities (such as when stakeholders or subject-matter experts are reviewing project outputs), encourage people to take time for themselves. Finally, when building your project schedules, incorporate adequate time for people to maintain healthy family and personal lives.
- *Share information.* To the extent that it is appropriate, let project team members know what's going on—what's behind the scenes and what's motivating the tough decisions that you, your sponsor, and senior managers are making. This lets team members know that you trust them and that they aren't simply victims of decisions made on high, but valued members of the inner circle.
- *Provide feedback on performance.* Sometimes during the project things can get pretty hectic, so it's easy to forget to provide team members with feedback on their performance. Regularly evaluating performance and providing feedback not only provides you with the opportunity to help them improve their contributions, it lets project team members know that someone is noticing when they do a good job—that their work matters.
- *Provide opportunities for involvement in decision making.* People like to feel that they have a hand in determining their own destinies. Whenever it's appropriate, involve project team members in making decisions that relate to the structure and shape of deliverables they are creating, the tasks they are completing, or the review processes that their part of the project will undergo. Indeed, if your project team members are highly skilled experts, it only makes sense to incorporate their perspectives in all decisions that relate to their contributions.
- *Provide independence.* By giving project team members the opportunity to work independently, you let them know that they are trusted. This can be powerfully motivating and is a simple means of recognizing their past and present contributions.
- *Provide celebrations.* Some project managers go so far as to have postproject awards

ceremonies, providing plaques or certificates of achievement for outstanding project accomplishments. For others, especially when the team is working on a difficult or long-running project, it can be enough simply to take people out to dinner or a special lunch at the end of a project phase or to celebrate completion of a noteworthy project milestone.

- *Provide flexibility in the work.* In many cases, especially relating to the contributions of individual professionals on a project team, the hours to be worked, the location of work (e.g., in a den or home-based office as opposed to an office building), and the moment-to-moment sequence of work chores may be considered discretionary. If, for example, a top project contributor would like to take two days off in the middle of the week and is able to complete her project contributions on schedule by working at home on Saturday and Sunday, then she should be able to do so. When project managers allow team members flexibility in the way they organize and perform the details of their work, they are not only showing that they trust the team members, but are openly recognizing their value and contributions.

- *Provide increased responsibility.* Giving a project team member increased responsibilities can be a powerful sign of trust and proof of his value to the project. What's more, when applied judiciously, this practice may also be a way for the project manager to more effectively delegate some responsibilities. (Note: The increased responsibilities, if they are to be truly used as recognition, should be meaningful and not simply amount to a greater volume of mundane or tedious chores.)

Source: Adapted from Bob Nelson and Peter Economy, *Managing for Dummies* (Foster City, CA: IDG Books, 1996), pp. 337-340.

WHAT A VETERAN PROJECT MANAGER MIGHT DO

What a seasoned project manager might do to complete this step is not substantially different from what a novice should do. He or she would simply have more experience and the ability to anticipate problems based on early warning signs.

A veteran project manager is also likely to have a strong network of people, both on and off the project team, with whom he or she can have an informal lunch or quick conversation in order to keep in touch with project status in a low-profile way. This can help the project manager identify problems before they become too large to handle.

PITFALLS AND CAUTIONS

Novice project managers are often tempted to hover or peer too frequently over the shoulders of team members who are trying to execute their assigned responsibilities. At this point in the project, it is appropriate simply to get people started and get out of their way so they can do their jobs, gathering status information as planned.

On the other hand, novice project managers sometimes can be overly impressed by the expertise or experience of the people they are trying to manage. This can result in the project manager's blindly trusting that everything is going well, without examining project outputs. In such situations, it is valuable to remember that even experts need to be provided with clear instructions about what results are expected of them, and when.

In most cases, the project manager should try to match his or her inspection style to the person being inspected. Some people like more attention, while others prefer to be left alone for long periods of time. When deciding how often and by what methods you will make your inspection, you should take into consideration the preferences of the team members as well as the project management requirements.

For tips on controlling project activities, see the next Action Item: Control Project Activities.

FOR MORE INFORMATION . . .

See PMI's *PMBOK* item 4.2., Project Plan Execution; item 9.3, Team Development; item 10.2, Information Distribution; item 12.3, Solicitation; item 12.4, Source Selection; and item 12.5, Contract Administration.

CONTROLLING

Controlling involves comparing actual performance with planned performance. In other words, are you doing exactly what you planned to do? If you discover deviations from the plan (often called *variances*), you must analyze these variances and figure out alternative actions that will get the project back on track. You can then decide which alternative is best and take appropriate corrective action. Controlling involves several subprocesses:

- Progress reporting
- Overall change control
- Scope change control
- Cost control
- Quality control
- Quality assurance
- Risk control

For more details, see the expanded description of this process in Part II: Your Essential Project Actions.

The following Action Item supports the process of controlling:

- Action Item: Control Project Activities

Action Item: Control Project Activities

Assignment

Take steps to control the project's activities.

Desired Outputs

- Inspections of deliverables
- Decision to accept inspected deliverables
- Corrective actions
- Rework of deliverables
- Adjustments to work process
- Updates to project plan and scope
- Revised deliverables' estimates
- Revised schedule estimates
- Revised cost estimates
- Updates to risk management plan
- Updates to activity list or work breakdown structure
- List of lessons learned
- Improved quality
- Completed evaluation checklists (if applicable)

Background Information

Controlling the progress of the project includes measuring results to identify variances or deviations from the approved plan. When significant variances are observed (such as those that jeopardize the project objectives), adjustments to the plan are made by repeating the appropriate project planning processes. In addition, controlling progress includes taking preventative action in anticipation of possible problems. Finally, controlling sometimes results in reworking deliverables or adjusting the work process to achieve the desired results.[88]

It is difficult to provide generic background information about how to control specific project activities or phases. "Best practices" of a particular industry as well as widely differing project deliverables dictate all sorts of different approaches to project control. However, some general control procedures may be described.

In a nutshell, controlling begins when progress reports (documents describing progress related to schedules, cost estimates, and so forth) and deliverables are inspected to note deviations from the plan. If deviations are noted, the project manager may decide to rework the deliverables, revise the project plan (budget, schedule, and so forth), or intervene to get things back on track. Note that the project should be inspected with all aspects of the plan in mind, not just the planned deliverables, costs, and budget. This means that the planned risk control and quality control measures should also be applied when controlling the overall project.

Guidelines for Controlling a Project Phase

Instructions: Follow these steps to control a particular project phase or activity. You may use the check boxes to mark items as completed.

Step 1: Review the project plan carefully and get a clear picture of what the desired results of this phase are in terms of deliverables, schedules, costs, quality, and minimized risk.

☐ Project plan is reviewed; overall desired results are identified.

Step 2: Prepare to inspect results of the phase (work product, deliverables). To make these preparations, consult the detailed project plan and do the following:

- Locate all lists of criteria that may be applied to inspect the quality and completeness of the deliverables in the light of the time frame you are examining. (For example, if this is the third week in January, examine the plan to find out exactly what stage of development and at what quality level the deliverables should be the third week in January.)
- Locate milestones and schedule events that relate to the time frame in which you are conducting the inspection. (For example, if this is the third week in January, examine calendars and schedules to see what should be accomplished around this week.)
- Locate the budget. Note particularly if there are expected dollar amounts that should be expended in the current time frame.
- Locate contractors' proposals or contracts. Note exactly what they have committed to supply (deliverables, reports, etc.).
- Locate the risk management plan, if one has been created. Note particularly whether any of the ongoing events or upcoming events are identified in the risk management plan as particularly vulnerable to risk.

Step 3: Inspect project results by examining actual deliverables to date, discussing results to date with project team members, and reviewing progress reports.

☐ Deliverables are examined.
☐ Results are discussed with team members responsible.
☐ Progress reports are reviewed.

Step 4: Decide whether to accept the inspected deliverables and work processes or to take corrective action such as:

- Insisting on rework of deliverables to conform to specifications
- Making adjustments to work process to prevent deviations

☐ Decision to accept or require rework is made.
☐ Decision to modify work process is made.

Step 5: As appropriate, make updates to the project plan and scope, including:

- Revised deliverables' estimates
- Revised schedule estimates
- Revised cost estimates
- Updates to the risk management plan

Step 6: Create a list of lessons learned that describes the ways subsequent project activities must be modified in order to prevent difficulties encountered.

☐ List of lessons learned is created.

Step 7: Complete evaluation checklists (if applicable) and file them as part of the official project records.

☐ Evaluations are completed and filed.

Guidelines for Keeping Things Moving: A To-Do List and Items to Help You Execute, Control, and Close Out Your Project

Instructions: After your project plan is approved and you are up and running, you can use the checklist below and the related items to help you keep things moving according to your plan.

Go through this list at least weekly for each project you are managing.

■ **CHECK YOUR PROJECT'S SCOPE.**

Refresh your memory about your project's goals and boundaries. In particular, make sure you have a clear picture of what the desired results should be at this point relative to deliverables, schedule costs, quality, and so on.

See Worksheet: Project Scope Statement under Action Item: Describe Project Scope if you don't already have a formal scope statement.

■ **CHECK YOUR DELIVERABLES.**

Analyze the status of each project deliverable. Are they evolving as planned? If appropriate:

1. Locate *lists of quality criteria* that may be applied to inspect the quality and completeness of the deliverables at this stage of the project.
2. Check *contractors' proposals or contracts* to make sure you know what they should be supplying at this point.
3. Inspect all project deliverables.
4. Decide whether to accept inspected deliverables or to require rework.

See Worksheet: Project Deliverables' Status Analyzer.

■ **CHECK YOUR SCHEDULE.**

Examine your milestones, key dates, and critical path. Are you where you need to be?

■ **ANALYZE VARIANCES (DEVIATIONS FROM PLAN) BY COMPARING ESTIMATED TO ACTUAL.**

1. Are activities taking longer than planned? (Are you exceeding estimates of duration?)
2. Are you using more resource hours than you planned?
3. Are your actual costs exceeding your estimated costs?
4. If minor variances are discovered (variances that can be resolved easily without changing the plan or scope), then resolve them.
5. If major variances are discovered (variances that change the scope or constitute significant project issues), then handle them as described in the steps below.

See Worksheet: Variance Analyzer.

■ **ADDRESS SCOPE CHANGES.**

1. Identify changes in scope (changes in deliverables, schedule, costs, etc.).
2. Handle scope changes, if necessary.

See Guidelines: Handling Scope Change and *Worksheet: Project Scope Change Order.*

■ **LIST, TRACK, AND TRY TO RESOLVE OPEN ISSUES.**

1. Make a list of all the unresolved issues, *or*
2. Revisit the list of open issues from the last inspection period and try to resolve them.

See Worksheet: Project Issue Tracker.

■ **REVISIT POTENTIAL PROJECT RISKS.**

2. Locate the Risk Management Plan, if one has been created.
2. Note particularly whether any of the ongoing events or upcoming events are identified in the risk management plan as particularly vulnerable to risk.

■ **REPORT PROJECT STATUS.**

1. After completing the checks above, if you haven't already done so, talk to your team members and determine their perspective on project status.
2. Create and circulate a project status report.

See Worksheet: The Project Status Report.

■ **DRIVE FOR CLOSE-OUT OF ACTIVITIES AND SIGN-OFF OF DELIVERABLES AS APPROPRIATE.**

1. Ask yourself, "What activities can I close out? Which deliverables can I get formally approved and signed off?"
2. Prepare and get signatures on sign-off forms as appropriate.

See Worksheet: Sample Project Sign-off Form under *Action Item: Close Out Project Activities.*

■ **DECIDE WHETHER IT'S NECESSARY TO KILL THE PROJECT; THEN DO SO IF APPROPRIATE.**
See Appendix E: Guidelines: When to Kill the Project.

- **CREATE A LIST OF LESSONS LEARNED.**

  Create a list of lessons learned that describes the ways subsequent project activities must be modified in order to prevent the difficulties encountered up to this point.

- **COMPLETE APPROPRIATE EVALUATION CHECKLISTS.**

  Complete evaluation checklists, if applicable, and file them as part of the official project records.

WORKSHEET: Project Deliverables' Status Analyzer

Deliverable:			As of:		
	Work Product (Deliverable) Status	*Quality Level*	*Schedule Status*	*Team Status*	*Cost Status*
Ideal State					
Current State					
Issues/Obstacles/Risks					
Ways to Remove Issues/Obstacles/Risks					
To Do *What*					
Who					
Deadline					
To Do *What*					
Who					
Deadline					

WORKSHEET: Variance Analyzer

Instructions: This worksheet will help you analyze variances (deviations from plan) by comparing estimated to actual. Enter the name of a project phase ("Phase:") and list all related project activities. Next, examine your project plan. Then, for each activity list the estimated duration, total labor hours, and costs (Est. Dur., Est. Hrs. and Est. $$) allocated for completing that activity. Next, enter the actual time elapsed (Act. Dur.), actual labor hours consumed (Act. Hrs.), and actual costs (Act. $$) related to complete each activity. Finally, compare all actuals (Act. . .) with estimates (Est. . .) to determine all the variances from plan (Var. . .).

For example, if you estimated an activity to be 10 days and it required only 8 days, then you have a positive variance of 2 days for the duration of the activity. Alternately, if you estimated that an activity might consume 80 labor hours and it actually required 100 labor hours, then you have a negative variance of 20 hours for the activity's labor hours. As these examples illustrate, you should subtract *Actual* from *Estimated* to determine *Variance*. To complete the analysis, note any explanations for the cause of the variance.

Phase: *Activities:*	Est. Dur.	Act. Dur.	Var. Dur.	Est. Hrs.	Act. Hrs.	Var. Hrs.	Est. $$	Act. $$	Var. $$	*Explanation*

Guidelines for Handling Scope Change

Background: Scope change may be defined as any addition, reduction, or modification to the deliverables or work process as outlined in your original project plan. Change of scope is normal—it's not necessarily a problem. In fact, scope changes can be beneficial when they allow the project team to respond sensibly to changing conditions that exist outside the project. This can help ensure that project deliverables remain relevant.

Project managers should approach changes of scope in a business-like (as opposed to emotional) fashion. The steps below outline a systematic process for dealing with scope change.

1. ***Stay calm.*** Remind yourself that the original project scope documents were created at a time when you knew less than you know now. Given the new knowledge and circumstances, you need to modify your plan. This will likely result in your having to ask for more time, more resources, more money, and other concessions from your sponsors or stakeholders. Realize that you'll simply need to analyze the situation and make a solid case for your new requirements. So there's no need to panic.

2. ***Pinpoint the exact change.*** Clearly and dispassionately state the exact scope of the change that is required.

3. ***Analyze the impact of the change.*** Specify how the change will affect:
   - Schedule
   - Quality of the finished product
   - Costs
   - Project team assignments, including level of effort
   - Other deliverables, including amount and quality

4. ***Discuss the impact with your project team.*** Assemble relevant team members and brainstorm alternatives for handling the change with as little impact as possible.

5. ***Report the impact to the sponsor.*** Make sure the sponsor is aware of implications of the change by discussing the change with the sponsor and his or her key stakeholder-recommenders.

6. ***Update the project scope statement and overall plan.*** Make an addendum or a complete revision, if appropriate, of the project schedule, work breakdown structure, scope description, and so on. Make sure you note all of the conditions that led to the change, the people who discussed alternatives, and the people who selected the recommended alternative. Document it; get it in writing.

7. ***Obtain written sponsor approval*** of the change and the corresponding revised plan. To guard against "amnesia" on the part of the sponsor, make sure the sponsor signs a document acknowledging the scope change and its rationale.

WORKSHEET: Project Scope Change Order

Project Name: _____ **Date:** _____

Project Manager: _____

Project Tracking Number: _____ **Change No.:** _____

Summary of Change:

Rationale for Change:

Brief overview of the impact of this change on . . .

- Project schedule:

- Quality of deliverables:

- Costs:

- Stakeholders and/or core team members:

- Other deliverables, including amount and quality:

Change approved by (signatures):

Sponsor: _____ **Date:** _____

Project Manager: _____ **Date:** _____

Other: _____ **Date:** _____

WORKSHEET: Project Issue Tracker

Project:				As of:			
Description of Issue or Required Action	*Date Named*	*Status (open or closed)*	*Deadline to Resolve*	*Date Closed*	*Internal Team Member Responsible*	*External Team Member Responsible*	*Immediate To-Do Items, Comments, or How Resolved*

WORKSHEET: The Project Status Report

Project Title:

Date:

Author:

Accomplishments Since Last Report
(Deliverables completed, milestones attained, decisions made, issues resolved, etc.)

-
-
-
-
-
-

Upcoming Activities
(What the team must focus on accomplishing throughout the next reporting period.)

-
-
-
-
-
-

Summary of Issues, Concerns, and Recommended Actions
(What issues or concerns are unresolved? Include recommended actions for each.)

-
-
-
-
-
-

Comments
(Miscellaneous comments, public praise for extra effort, announcements, etc.)

-
-
-
-
-
-

What a Veteran Project Manager Might Do

What a project management professional might do to complete this step is not substantially different from what a novice should do. He or she would simply have more experience and thus may have the ability to probe deeply when making inspections, identifying more between-the-lines issues. He or she may also be more likely to come up with quick "work-arounds" to keep the project on track.

A project management professional might also employ powerful project management software to allow fast and easy "zoom in" on detailed aspects of the project plan. Such software might also help "zoom out" to the big-picture view so that the manager can see ways in which the potential corrective actions might affect the project as a whole. Finally, it might allow the project manager to play "what if?" by entering data related to a potential corrective procedure and tracking the effects on a revised project plan.

Pitfalls and Cautions

It's sometimes difficult to control project activities without appearing to micromanage or butt in on the efforts of the professionals who are working on the project. If people feel they are being overmanaged, they can lose the sense of ownership for their work. For this reason, it is important that the project manager conduct only those inspections that are expected by staff members.

In addition, when providing instructions for correcting deviations, it is important that the project manager focus on the work to be performed and avoid personal comments about the performer. Feedback should be task related, clearly justified, and unemotional, such as, "According to the blueprints, this wall was to be reinforced. It is clearly not reinforced, so it will have to be rebuilt." Feedback should not take the form of personal criticism, such as "Can't you read blueprints? This wall was supposed to be reinforced! You ignored the requirements, so now you will have to rebuild it!" Having to correct a mistake is one thing, being made to feel like a fool is quite another. If you are to maintain a productive work environment, your inspection and feedback techniques must be professional, unemotional, and respectful of the efforts made by the person who performed the job.

Finally, remember that you get the kinds of results you reward. This means that if people are doing a good job and your inspections show it, you should spend the time and energy to publicly praise and reward them. This not only lets everyone know you are paying attention, but it shows other team members that extra effort can be worthwhile.

For More Information . . .

See PMI's *PMBOK* item 4.3, Overall Change Control; item 5.5, Scope Change Control; item 6.5, Schedule Control; item 7.4, Cost Control; item 8.3, Quality Control; item 8.2, Quality Assurance; item 10.3, Performance Reporting; and item 11.4, Risk Response Control.

Closing

Because projects are temporary endeavors, projects and project phases must eventually come to an end. But who is to say when a project or phase has ended? More important, how do you know when to stop expending effort and money on a project or project phase?

Projects typically involve many stakeholders, each of whom is likely to have an opinion about the suitability of deliverables. To help prevent disputes, it is necessary to set up a formal process by which the project or project phase may be declared officially completed. This formal process is called closing. *Closing* involves formalizing the acceptance of results and ending the project or phase. This includes several subprocesses:

- Scope verification
- Administrative closure or obtaining sign-off approval
- Contract close-out

Note that clear-cut and effective closing is based on the formal, approved project plan. The actual results achieved can be compared to the planned results, thus minimizing disputes over whether the deliverables are suitable.

For more details, see the expanded description of this process in Part II: Your Essential Project Actions.

The following Action Item supports the process of closing:

- Action Item: Close Out Project Activities

Action Item: Close Out Project Activities

Assignment

Complete the close-out of a particular phase or activity.

Desired Outputs

- Formal acceptance, documented in writing, that the sponsor has accepted the product of this phase or activity (may be conditional)
- Formal acceptance of contractor work products (deliverables) and updates to the contractor's files
- Updated project records prepared for archiving (may include updates to historical databases extending beyond the project to the overall program)
- A plan for follow-up and/or hand-off of project work products

Background Information

Projects are by definition temporary undertakings. Therefore, project phases must each have a specific end. These end points are typically identified by formal close-out procedures. At the end of the project phase, the phase is closed out by:

- Scope verification—ensuring that all identified project deliverables have been completed satisfactorily[89]
- Administrative closure—generating, gathering, and disseminating information to formalize the completion of the phase (i.e., letting the world know it's done! by formal announcements, sign-offs, and so on)[90]
- Contract close-out—completion and settlement of the contracts with suppliers, including resolving any outstanding items[91]
- Plan for follow-up and/or hand-off—taking necessary steps to see that the sponsor or end user obtains the work product as planned

Guidelines for Closing Out a Project Phase

Instructions: Follow these steps to close out (bring to an "official" conclusion) a particular project phase or activity. You may use the check boxes to mark items as completed.

Step 1: Assemble the following documentation:

- Work breakdown structure (WBS)
- Progress reports
- Change requests
- Any planning documents that established the framework for performance measurement
- Detailed descriptions of the project's finished product (deliverables)
- Contractor correspondence relating to terms and conditions of performance, contract changes, or clarifications
- Contract changes
- Contractor payment requests

Step 2: Inspect to determine completion of the phase.

- Measure, examine, and test work product (deliverables) to ensure that results conform to requirements. This may include conducting walk-through examinations, audits, reviews, and so on.[92]
- Conduct a procurement audit to identify contractor successes and failures.[93]

Step 3: Conduct a project team review of successes, failures, lessons learned, methods or technologies developed that should be applied in other projects, and follow-up activities.[94] This is sometimes called a project *postmortem review*. (See Project Postmortem Review Questions.)

☐ Team review is conducted.

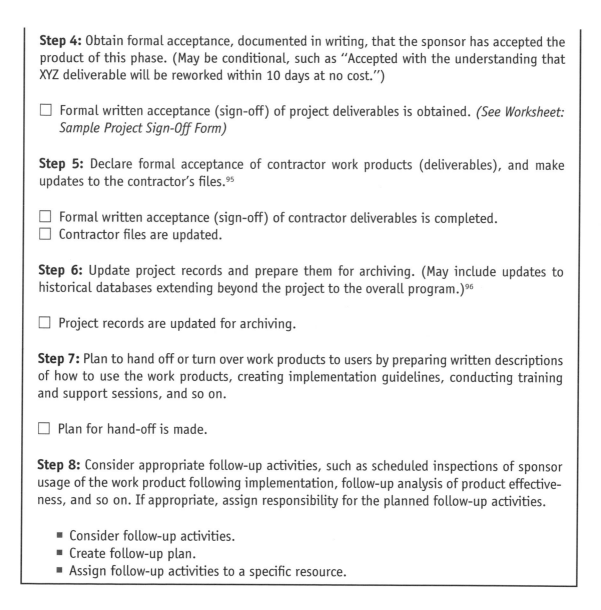

Step 4: Obtain formal acceptance, documented in writing, that the sponsor has accepted the product of this phase. (May be conditional, such as "Accepted with the understanding that XYZ deliverable will be reworked within 10 days at no cost.")

☐ Formal written acceptance (sign-off) of project deliverables is obtained. *(See Worksheet: Sample Project Sign-Off Form)*

Step 5: Declare formal acceptance of contractor work products (deliverables), and make updates to the contractor's files.[95]

☐ Formal written acceptance (sign-off) of contractor deliverables is completed.
☐ Contractor files are updated.

Step 6: Update project records and prepare them for archiving. (May include updates to historical databases extending beyond the project to the overall program.)[96]

☐ Project records are updated for archiving.

Step 7: Plan to hand off or turn over work products to users by preparing written descriptions of how to use the work products, creating implementation guidelines, conducting training and support sessions, and so on.

☐ Plan for hand-off is made.

Step 8: Consider appropriate follow-up activities, such as scheduled inspections of sponsor usage of the work product following implementation, follow-up analysis of product effectiveness, and so on. If appropriate, assign responsibility for the planned follow-up activities.

- Consider follow-up activities.
- Create follow-up plan.
- Assign follow-up activities to a specific resource.

PROJECT POSTMORTEM REVIEW QUESTIONS

It's important for project managers and team members to take stock at the end of a project and develop a list of lessons learned so that they don't repeat their mistakes in the next project. Typically such reviews are called *postproject reviews* or *postmortems*. We recommend a two-step process for conducting these reviews:

1. Prepare and circulate a whole bunch of specific questions about the project and give team members time to think about them and prepare their responses individually.
2. Hold a meeting and discuss the team's responses to the questions. The result of this discussion is often a list of lessons learned.

The benefit of the first step, done individually by team members, is that it allows the quieter, more analytical people to develop their responses to the questions without being interrupted by the more outgoing, vocal types who might otherwise dominate in the face-to-face meeting. Also, it allows everyone the time to create more thoughtful responses.

So what would be on the list of questions? We've provided some of our favorites below.

General Questions

1. Are you proud of our finished deliverables (project work products)? If yes, what's so good about them? If no, what's wrong with them?
2. What was the single most frustrating part of our project?
3. How would you do things differently next time to avoid this frustration?
4. What was the most gratifying or professionally satisfying part of the project?
5. Which of our methods or processes worked particularly well?
6. Which of our methods or processes were difficult or frustrating to use?
7. If you could wave a magic wand and change anything about the project, what would you change?
8. Did our stakeholders, senior managers, customers, and sponsors participate effectively? If not, how could we improve their participation?

Phase-Specific Questions

These will differ from project to project, depending on the life cycle and phases. The phases identified below are explained in the discussion of our generic Project Life Cycle in Part I.

Phase I: Determine Need and Feasibility

1. Did our needs/market analysis or feasibility study identify all the project deliverables that we eventually had to build? If not, what did we miss, and how can we be sure our future analyses don't miss such items?
2. Did our needs/market analysis or feasibility study identify unnecessary deliverables? If so, how can we be sure our future analyses don't make this mistake?
3. How could we have improved our need-feasibility or analysis phase?

Phase II: Create Project Plan

1. How accurate were our original estimates of the size and effort of our project? What did we over- or underestimate? (Consider deliverables, work effort, materials required, etc.)
2. How could we have improved our estimate of size and effort so that it was more accurate?
3. Did we have the right people assigned to all project roles? (Consider subject-

matter expertise, technical contributions, management, review and approval, and other key roles.) If no, how can we make sure that we get the right people next time?

4. Describe any early warning signs of problems that occurred later in the project. How should we have reacted to these signs? How can we be sure to notice these early warning signs next time?

5. Could we have completed this project without one or more of our vendors or contractors? If so, how?

6. Were our constraints, limitations, and requirements made clear to all vendors and contractors from the beginning? If not, how could we have improved our RFP or statement of need?

7. Were there any difficulties negotiating the vendor contract? How could these have been avoided?

8. Were there any difficulties setting up vendor paperwork (purchase orders, contracts, etc.) or getting the vendor started? How could these have been avoided?

9. List team members or stakeholders who were missing from the kickoff meeting or who were not involved early enough in our project. How can we avoid these oversights in the future?

10. Were all team and stakeholder roles and responsibilities clearly delineated and communicated? If not, how could we have improved these?

11. Were the deliverables' specifications, milestones, and specific schedule elements and dates clearly communicated? If not, how could we improve this?

Phase III: Create Specifications for Deliverables

1. Were you proud of our blueprints or other detailed design specifications? If not, how could we have improved these?

2. Did all the important project players have creative input into the creation of the design specifications? If not, whom were we missing, and how can we ensure their involvement next time?

3. Did those who reviewed the design specifications provide timely and meaningful input? If not, how could we have improved their involvement and the quality of their contributions?

4. How could we have improved our work process for creating deliverables' specifications?

[Insert your own deliverables-specific questions here.]

Phase IV: Create Deliverables

1. Were you proud of our deliverables? If not, how could we have improved these?

2. Did all the important project players have creative input into the creation of

the deliverables? If not, whom were we missing, and how can we ensure their involvement next time?

3. Did those who reviewed the deliverables provide timely and meaningful input? If not, how could we have improved their involvement and the quality of their contributions?

4. How could we have improved our work process for creating deliverables?

[Insert your own deliverables-specific questions here.]

Phase V: Test and Implement Deliverables

1. Were the members of our test audience truly representative of our target audience? If not, how could we ensure better representation in the future?

2. Did the test facilities, equipment, materials, and support people help to make the test an accurate representation of how the deliverables will be used in the real world? If not, how could we have improved on these items?

3. Did we get timely, high-quality feedback about how we might improve our deliverables? If not, how could we get better feedback in the future?

4. Was our implementation strategy accurate and effective? How could we improve this strategy?

5. Did our hand-off of deliverables to the user/customer/sponsor represent a smooth and easy transition? If not, how could we have improved this process?

[Insert your own deliverables-specific questions here.]

WORKSHEET: Sample Project Sign-Off Form

Project Name:

I have reviewed the following deliverables as of the date identified below:

-
-
-
-
-

I have found these deliverables to meet with my approval, with the following exceptions:

-
-
-

I hereby give my approval to proceed with the evolution of these deliverables to the next stage of development in order to meet the project objectives in a timely fashion.

I understand that any changes (additions, deletions, or modifications) to the fundamental structure, underlying design, or the specific features of these deliverables might result in:

- Slippage of the completion date for these deliverables
- Additional resource requirements
- Additional costs

_____ **[Signature]**

[Name, position]
[Organization name]

Date: _____

What a Veteran Project Manager Might Do

What a seasoned project manager might do to complete this step is not substantially different from what a novice should do. He or she would simply have more experience and thus may be better able to navigate the paperwork.

Pitfalls and Cautions

Toward the end of a project or project phase, people can become weary and eager to finish and move on. It's tempting for those who created the deliverables or provided the services simply to hand them over and leave. What's more, many of the professionals who make up the project team are often already booked on their next project and have begun work elsewhere. However, since projects nearly always involve a legal obligation (a contract of some sort and a written proposal), it's essential that formal close-out procedures be followed carefully.

As project manager you need to make sure that everyone delivers what they promised and that the sponsor has formally approved the results. In this way, you can be sure that the phase or project is really complete and there are no loose ends for you to tie up when everyone else has moved on.

For More Information . . .

See PMI's *PMBOK* items 5.4, Scope Verification; item 10.4, Administrative Closure; and item 12.6, Contract Close-Out.

See PMI's *Negotiating and Contracting for Project Management* by Penny Cavendish and Martin D. Martin.

See PMI's *Contract Administration for the Project Manager* by Martin D. Martin, C. Claude Teagarden, and Charles F. Lambreth.

Tips for Managing Experts Outside Your Expertise

Occasionally you may find yourself on a project team that includes experts about whose specialties you know absolutely nothing. Don't panic—this is a normal part of management, something that every project manager eventually faces. In fact, in today's downsized and projectized organizations, people from many different backgrounds are increasingly asked to work together in all sorts of unanticipated ways. So, for example, marketing folks are likely to be shoulder-to-shoulder with engineers on the same project. To make matters worse, project managers are usually expected to make their own contributions to the project from their particular field of expertise—they don't have the time to develop expertise in everyone else's fields. So it is inevitable that new, part-time, ad hoc project managers find themselves trying to manage the activities of someone who is a specialist in a field about which the manager knows little or nothing.

Yes, it's intimidating. But there are some simple steps you can take to make your work with these experts more effective.

Symptoms

Here are some symptoms that you may be in over your head when it comes to understanding what an expert on your project team does for a living:

- You are uneasy when attempting to plan specific activities or make inspections of outputs associated with the expert's project responsibilities.

- Nearly all of the expert's sentences include at least one term or acronym that you don't understand.
- The expert sometimes leans forward when talking to you and speaks slowly, as though you are not very bright.
- In meetings, when you are presenting descriptions of project activities and come to what the expert's part of the project will involve, the expert rolls his or her eyes or acts puzzled by your description—or the expert continually interrupts you to explain to your colleagues, "What he [or she] really means is . . ."
- When interacting with you, the expert avoids eye contact, mumbles acronym-filled phrases, and shakes his or her head in frustration.

IS AN ATTITUDE ADJUSTMENT REQUIRED?

Face it. You can't be an expert in all fields. But with the proper attitude, you can make working with experts a more pleasant and productive experience. Here are some attitudes or mind-shifts you should consider adopting when working with experts outside your area of expertise:

- Think of yourself as a mere project facilitator, not the supreme, all-knowing project commander. In this way, you won't expect yourself to know everything about each of the professions represented on the team.
- As facilitator, expect to help people get resources when they need them and to lend people a hand when they get stuck in administrivia. This doesn't require expertise in their field. You simply have to ask them what they need and figure out how to help them get it.
- Keep in mind that ignorance (lack of knowledge) is not the same as stupidity. You are undoubtedly a successful, intelligent person. You simply lack knowledge in a particular subject area.
- Expect to learn some new things about the expert's field, but expect to remain ignorant of much of the field.
- Remember that first and foremost you are responsible for achieving project deliverables on time and within budget. You are most likely not responsible for knowing what the experts know.
- Readily (though not constantly) admit when you don't know something. You'll be surprised how willing many experts are to become your teacher.

TIPS FOR WORKING WITH EXPERTS OUTSIDE YOUR AREA OF EXPERTISE

Try some of these techniques for working with experts outside your area of expertise:

- Get them involved early on in the project, and ask them to help you plan, in detail, all the activities associated with their part of the project.

- Openly express your respect for their professional judgment, and frequently seek their opinions.
- Let them know you aren't pretending to know their profession.
- Don't try to micromanage their specific actions. Instead, focus on their results by repeatedly referring to the deliverables' specifications and formal statement of project scope.
- Ask them to provide you with overview information relating to their field. (These might take the form of handbooks, primers, slide presentations, promotional videos from professional associations, and so on.)
- Ask them to describe for you the essential characteristics of finished products and work processes in their field. In other words, find out where their professional values lie and in what situations you can expect them to fight for these values.
- Single out a friendly expert, and ask him or her to help you learn the jargon, acronyms, and underlying values of the profession. Ask this person to coach you or help you prepare for difficult meetings with his or her colleagues.
- Try to establish some basis of commonality. Go to lunch and get acquainted. Do you both enjoy hiking? The opera? Your children? Remember, when you regard each other as people and not merely as robots performing job roles, you are both more likely to spend the energy necessary to achieve understanding.

```
┌──────────────┐
│  APPENDIX B  │
└──────┬───────┘
       │
       │
```

GLOSSARY OF
PROJECT
MANAGEMENT
TERMS

This glossary contains many common PM terms, but it is by no means exhaustive. If you are looking for comparisons among conflicting definitions, for definitions of relatively esoteric PM terms, or for a frequently updated glossary, please visit Max Wideman's *Comparative Glossary of Common Project Management Terms* online at: http://www.pmforum.org/library/glossary/index.htm

Activity   A unit of work performed to complete a project. An activity typically takes time (duration) and expends resources. Activities are often broken down into a series of individual, but related, tasks.

Actual Cost of Work Performed (ACWP)   The total costs that were incurred (direct and indirect) in accomplishing work during a given time period.

Actual Finish Date   The date that work was actually ended on an activity.

Actual Start Date   The date that work was actually begun on a particular activity.

Baseline   A fixed project schedule that represents the original plan for the project (including approved changes). The baseline is a yardstick against which the actual project plan is measured to detect deviations. Baselines can take the form of cost baselines, time or schedule baselines, and so on.

Budgeted Cost of Work Performed (BCWP)   The sum total of all approved cost estimates for project activities completed during a particular time period.

Budgeted Cost of Work Scheduled (BCWS)   The sum total of all approved cost estimates for project activities that are planned or scheduled to be performed during a particular time period.

Calendar   A project calendar lists time intervals in which activities or resources can or cannot be scheduled. A project usually has one default calendar for the normal workweek (Monday through Friday), but may have other calendars as well. Each calendar can be customized with its own holidays and extra workdays.

Calendar Unit   The smallest unit of time used in creating the project schedule (typically hours, days, or weeks).

Chart of Accounts   A numbering system used to label or categorize project costs. Typically, the project's chart of accounts is consistent with the overall organization's chart of accounts.

Closing or Closing Out   Obtaining formal approval of the outputs of an activity, a phase, or the project as a whole. Typically project records are updated and deliverables are handed off.

Code of Accounts   A numbering system used to identify each component of the project's work breakdown structure.

Contingency Planning   The process by which a management plan is created to address certain potential project risks.

Control   The process of comparing actual performance with planned performance, analyzing the differences, and taking the appropriate corrective action. In addition, controlling involves updating the scope and plan as they change.

Critical Activity   Any activity that is on the project's critical path. A critical activity has zero or negative float. It must be finished on time or the whole project will fall behind schedule. (Noncritical activities have float or slack time and are not on the critical path. Supercritical activities have negative float.)

Critical Path   In the project's network diagram, the critical path is that path (or linked set of activities) which takes the most time to complete. All activities on the critical path must be completed on time; a delay in any activity on the critical path causes a delay in the completion of the project. There may be more than one critical path, depending on durations and the way work flow is organized.

Critical Path Method (CPM)   A method of determining project duration by analyzing the network diagram, finding the critical path, and making certain schedule calculations. CPM typically calculates the start and finish dates in two passes. The first pass calculates early start-and-finish dates from the earliest start date forward. The second pass calculates the late start-and-finish activities from the latest finish date backward. The difference between the pairs of start-and-finish dates for each task is the float or slack time for the task. An advantage of this method is the fine-tuning that can be done to accelerate the project. After the initial calculation, the project manager can shorten various critical path activities, then check the schedule to see how it is affected by the changes. By experimenting in this manner, the optimal project schedule can be determined. (Project management software can greatly simplify CPM analysis by automating the forward and backward calculations and then graphically depicting the critical path. In fact, on larger projects, such calculations would be almost impossible if done manually.)

Deliverable   Any measurable, tangible, verifiable output that must be produced to complete the project. Deliverables take two forms: interim outputs (such as video scripts, floor plans, or marketing analyses) and final deliverables associated with these interim outputs (such as the completed video presentation, the finished building, or a completed product marketing plan).

Duration The period of time over which a project task or activity takes place. *See also* Effort.

Duration Compression Shortening the project's overall schedule by assigning more resources to perform some activities.

Early Finish The earliest calculated date on which an activity can end. It is based on the activity's Early Start, which depends on the finish of predecessor activities and the activity's duration. Most project management software calculates early dates with a forward pass from the beginning of the project to the end.

Early Start The earliest calculated date on which an activity can begin. It is dependent on when all predecessor activities finish. Most project management software calculates early dates with a forward pass from the beginning of the project to the end.

Earned Value A method for quantifying and analyzing project performance by comparing the amount of work that was planned with what was actually accomplished. This allows the analyst to determine if cost and schedule are progressing as planned.

Effort (or Work) The amount of labor required to complete an activity. Effort is usually expressed as person-hours or person-days.

Elapsed Time The total number of calendar days (excluding nonworkdays such as weekends or holidays) that is needed to complete an activity.

Exception Report A project report that shows only major deviations from the original plan (rather than all deviations).

Executing Performing the activities of a project as planned; creating work results, making progress reports, and initiating change requests.

Fast Tracking The process by which the project schedule is compressed by doing some or all activities in parallel instead of in linear sequence.

Finish Date The calendar date at which an activity is to be completed.

Finish Float The amount of excess time an activity has at its finish before a successor activity must start. This is the difference between the start date of the predecessor and the finish date of the current activity, using the early or late schedule. (Early and late dates are not mixed.) This may be referred to as *slack time*. All floats are calculated when a project has its schedule computed.

Finish-to-Finish Lag The minimum amount of time that must pass between the finish of one activity and the finish of its successors. If the predecessor's finish is delayed, the successor activity may have to be slowed or halted to allow the specified time period to pass. Finish-to-finish lags are often used with start-to-start lags.

Finish-to-Start Lag The minimum amount of time that must pass between the finish of one activity and the start of its successors. The finish-to-start lag is zero. If the predecessor's finish is delayed, the successor activity's start will have to be delayed. In most cases, finish-to-start lags are not used with other lag types.

Finishing Activity The last activity that must be completed before a project can be considered finished. This activity is not a predecessor to any other activity—it has no successors.

Float Sometimes called *downtime, slack time,* or *path float,* float is the amount of time that an activity may be delayed from its start without delaying the entire project.

Free Float The excess time available before the start of the following activity, assuming that both activities start on their early start date.

Functional Manager A manager who is responsible for activities in a particular department or organizational function, such as accounting, advertising, and manufacturing.

Functional Organization An organization structure in which staff members are grouped hierarchically by their expertise or area of specialization, such as accounting, advertising, and manufacturing.

Gantt (Bar) Chart A graphic display of activity durations. Activities are listed with other tabular information on the left side, with time intervals over the bars. Activity durations are shown in the form of horizontal bars, which are proportionally longer or shorter, depicting relative differences in days', weeks', or months' duration.

Goal A broad result toward which the project team directs its efforts, but which is less quantifiable and measurable than is a specific deliverable. For example, one project goal may be to increase the opportunities for shopping in a particular neighborhood. A related deliverable would be the creation of a 25,000-square-foot retail shopping space.

Hammock A hammock groups activities, milestones, or other hammocks together for reporting.

Histogram A graphic display of resource usage over a period of time. Usually created by project management software, histograms allow the user to see overused or underused resources. In project management software, the resource usage is displayed in colored vertical bars. The ideal level for a resource on the screen is indicated by another color (typically red). The vertical height is produced by the value specified in the maximum usage field of the resource label window. (The printed histogram uses a horizontal line to display the maximum usage set in the resource label window.) If the resource bar extends beyond the red area for any given day, resources need to be leveled (or spread out) for a more balanced allocation. The resource histograms should be checked after resources are assigned to the project activities.

Initiating The process by which a project or project phase or activity is begun. Typically, initiating involves demonstrating project need and feasibility and obtaining authorization to begin.

Lag   The time delay between the start or finish of an activity and the start or finish of its successors.

Late Finish   In the critical path method, late finish dates are defined as the latest dates by which an activity can finish to avoid causing delays in the project. Many project management software packages calculate late dates with a backward pass from the end of the project to the beginning.

Late Start   In the critical path method, late start dates are defined as the latest dates by which an activity can start to avoid causing delays in the project. Many project management software packages calculate late dates with a backward pass from the end of the project to the beginning.

Lead   An overlap between activities in that the start of a task precedes the finish of its predecessor.

Master Schedule   A summary schedule that identifies all major activities and key milestones.

Matrix Organization   Any organizational structure in which project managers share responsibility with the functional managers for directing the work of people assigned to the project.

Micro-Scheduling   The scheduling of activities with durations of less than one day (in hours or fractional days).

Milestone   A significant event in the project, usually completion of a major deliverable. Milestones differ from project to project depending on the type of deliverables the project is designed to create. In project management software, a milestone is an activity that has been assigned zero duration (usually marking the end of an activity or phase).

Monte Carlo Analysis   A mathematical assessment method that performs a simulation of the project several times in order to calculate a distribution of potential results.

Multi-Project Analysis   Used to analyze the impact and interaction of activities and resources whose progress affects the progress of a group of projects. In particular, multi-project analysis is important when individual projects are sharing resources (people or equipment), since such analysis can help prevent overbooking. Multi-project analysis can also be used for composite reporting on projects having no dependencies or resources in common.

Near-Critical Activity   An activity that has very little total float.

Negative Float   Indicates activities must start before their predecessors finish in order to meet a target finish date. Negative float occurs when the difference between the late dates and the early dates (start or finish) of an activity is negative. In this situation, the late dates are earlier than the early dates. This can happen when constraints (activity target dates or a project target finish date) are imposed on a project.

Network Analysis   The process of identifying early and late start and finish dates for project activities. This is done with a forward and backward pass through the project. Many project management software tools check for loops in the network and issue an error message if one is found. The error message identifies the loop and all activities within it.

Network Diagram   A graphic representation of the sequence and relationship of project activities. Activity boxes (nodes) are connected by one-way arrows to indicate precedence. The first activity is placed on the left side of the diagram, with the last activity on the right side. Activity boxes are usually placed at different levels (not in a single row) to accommodate activities that are done simultaneously.

Network Path   A series of connected activities displayed in a network diagram.

Ongoing Operations   Those activities undertaken by an organization to routinely and repetitively generate the goods or services it has been set up to generate. Ongoing operations are distinct from projects, which are temporary, finite, and unique.

Parallel Activities   Two or more activities that can be done at the same time. This allows a project to be completed faster than if the activities were arranged serially or in a linear sequence.

Phase   A collection of logically related project activities, usually resulting in the completion of a major deliverable. By organizing project activities into a few major phases, it is easier to plan the project, discuss project events with team members, and analyze and track the project. The exact phases used in a project typically are established by professional standards in a particular industry.

Positive Float   The amount of time that an activity's start can be delayed without affecting the project completion date. An activity with positive float is not on the critical path and is called a *noncritical activity*. Most software packages calculate float time during schedule analysis. The difference between early and late dates (start or finish) determines the amount of float. Float time is shown at the end or the beginning of noncritical activities when a bar chart reflects both early and late schedules.

Precedence Notation   A means of describing project work flow. It is sometimes called *activity-on-node notation*. Each activity is assigned a unique identifier. Work flow direction is indicated by showing each of the activity's predecessors and their lag relationships. Graphically, precedence networks are represented by using descriptive boxes and connecting arrows to denote the flow of work.

Predecessor   An activity that must be completed (or be partially completed) before a specified activity can begin. The combination of all predecessors' and successors' relationships among the project activities forms a network. This network can be analyzed to determine the critical path and other project scheduling implications.

Program   A group of related projects whose outputs are typically integrated or coordinated and whose activities are managed together. Programs often include an element of an organization's ongoing activities.

Program Evaluation and Review Technique (PERT)   An event-oriented network analysis technique based on the use of a network diagram that shows dependencies between project tasks. In a PERT chart, activities are represented by boxes, or nodes, and relationships among activities are represented by lines that connect these nodes. In PERT analysis, each activity is assigned a best, worst, and most probable completion time estimate. These estimates are used to determine the average completion time. The average times are used to figure the critical path and the standard deviation of completion times for the entire project.

Project A temporary endeavor undertaken to create a unique product or service. Typically, a project is a one-time effort to accomplish an explicit objective by a specific time. Like the individual activities that make up the project, each project has a distinguishable start and finish and a time frame for completion. Each activity in the project will be monitored and controlled to determine its impact on other activities and projects. Unlike an organization's ongoing operations, a project must eventually come to a conclusion. The project is the largest discrete block of time and resources handled by most project management software.

Project Charter A document created and/or approved by upper management or the project sponsor that provides the project manager with the authority necessary to use organizational resources to complete project activities.

Project Life Cycle A collection of project phases whose name and number are determined by the control needs of the organization or organizations involved in the project. For example, the project life cycle of a motion picture project would include such phases as casting, scripting, shooting, editing, and so on. In contrast, the project life cycle for a home building project might include such phases as creating the blueprint, building the foundation, framing the walls, and so on. In each case, the project phases are unique to the industry and designed to achieve specific project deliverables. Also in each case, the project phases allow the project deliverables to evolve gradually and systematically. In this way, the project manager and the professionals involved on the team can inspect the deliverables as they are emerging in order to control the quality, timing, and cost. By using an industry-standard project life cycle, project managers can help ensure that deliverables will conform to recognized quality standards.

Project Management (PM) The application of knowledge, skills, tools, and techniques to project activities in order to meet or exceed stakeholder needs and expectations.

Project Management Professional (PMP) An individual certified as such by the Project Management Institute.

Project Management Software A computer application specifically designed to help plan and control project costs and schedules.

Project Plan A formal, approved document used to guide the execution and control of a project. The plan documents planning assumptions and decisions, and aids communication among stakeholders. In addition, the plan puts in writing the sponsor-approved scope, cost, and schedule baselines.

Project Planning Developing and updating the project plan. This involves describing project scope, defining and sequencing project activities, estimating durations of activities and resources required to complete them, and developing the schedule. In addition, planning involves estimating costs, building a budget, organizing and acquiring staff, organizing and selling the plan, and obtaining approval of the plan

Project Schedule   The planned calendar dates for completing activities and achieving milestones.

Project Team Members   The people who report to the project manager or work with him or her indirectly to accomplish project goals and complete project activities.

Projectized Organization   Any organizational structure in which project managers have all needed authority to assign priorities and to direct the work of people assigned to their projects.

Resource   Anything that is needed to complete an activity. This may include people, equipment, materials, facilities, and so on.

Resource-Based Duration   In project management software, a method of calculation that provides the option to determine activity duration, remaining duration, and percentage completed through resource usage. The resource requiring the greatest time to complete the specified amount of work on the activity will determine the duration of the activity.

Resource Leveling   The process of adjusting project schedules in order to minimize the peaks in daily resource usages. This is usually done when one or more resources are overallocated (assigned to work more hours in a day than they can work). In resource leveling, activities are moved within their available float to produce a new schedule. In project management software, resources and projects may be assigned leveling priorities. Some activities may not have any rescheduling flexibility due to lack of float. Software substantially simplifies this process, particularly when leveling on larger projects.

Schedule Variance   The difference between the scheduled completion date of an activity and the actual completion date of that activity.

Scheduled Finish Date   The date work was scheduled to end on an activity. The scheduled finish date typically falls between the early finish date and the late finish date.

Scheduled Start Date   The date work was scheduled to begin on an activity. The scheduled start date typically falls between the early start date and the late start date.

Scheduling   The process of determining when project activities will take place depending on defined durations and precedent activities. Schedule constraints specify when an activity should start or end based on duration, predecessors, external predecessor relationships, resource availability, or target dates.

Scope   The sum of the products (deliverables) and services to be provided as a project. The statement of project scope (a formal document) should include a list of deliverables, a list of project objectives, and a description of project success criteria, such as cost, quality, and schedule measures.

Scope Change   Any change made to the project scope. A scope change almost always leads to a revision of the project cost estimate or schedule, or both.

Sequence   The order in which activities will occur relative to each another. This establishes the priority and dependencies between activities. Successor and predecessor relationships are typically developed and displayed in a network format. This allows those involved in the project to visualize the work flow.

Slack   The amount of time a task can be delayed without delaying the project completion date.

Slippage   The amount of slack or float time used up by an activity due to a delayed start. If an activity without float is delayed, the entire project will slip.

SME (subject-matter expert)   A project participant who brings particular technical, legal, strategic, or other perspective in order to help improve the quality of deliverables.

Sponsor   The customer, client, final owner, or entity providing funds for the project. The sponsor also typically has the power to approve the use of other resources (such as staff members, equipment, and facilities) and stop the project.

Stakeholders   Individuals and organizations who are involved in, or may be affected by, project activities. Typical stakeholders include the project sponsor (the person or organization paying the bills and able to stop the project—sometimes called client, customer, or funder), suppliers, contractors, vendors, craftspeople, the project manager, government agencies, and the public.

Start Float   The amount of excess time an activity has between its early start and late start dates.

Starting Activity   An activity with no predecessors. It does not have to wait for any other activity to start.

Start-to-Start Lag   The minimum amount of time that must pass between the start of one activity and the start of its successors.

Statement of Work   A narrative description of all products or services to be provided by a contractor.

Subcritical Activity   An activity that has a float threshold value assigned to it by the project manager. When the activity reaches its float threshold, it is identified as being critical. Since this type of criticality is artificial, it normally does not have an impact on the project's end date.

Subnet or Subnetwork   The subdivision of a project network diagram into smaller components, each of which represents some form of subproject.

Subproject   A distinct group of activities that composes its own project, which in turn is a part of a larger project. Subprojects are sometimes summarized into a single activity to hide the detail and allow the activities to be viewed in summary form.

Successor   A successor is an activity whose start or finish depends on the start or finish of a predecessor activity.

Supercritical Activity   An activity that is behind schedule. It has been delayed to a point where its float is calculated to be a negative value. The negative float is representative of the number of schedule units by which an activity is behind schedule.

Target Finish—Activity   An imposed finish date for an activity. A target finish date typically represents predefined commitment dates. Most project management software will not schedule a late finish date later than the target finish date.

Target Finish—Project   An imposed completion date for a project as a whole. A target finish date is used if there is a predefined completion date. Most project management software will not schedule any late finish date later than the target finish date.

Target Start—Activity   An imposed starting date for an activity. Most project management software will not schedule an early start date earlier than the target start date.

Task   A subdivision of an activity; each activity may consist of several smaller tasks.

Time-Scaled Network Diagram   A project network diagram created so that the position of each activity represents its planned start date and finish date. In other words, it displays the relative durations of activities (like a Gantt chart) but includes the lines and nodes of a network diagram.

Total Float   The excess time available for an activity to be expanded or delayed without affecting the rest of the project—assuming it begins at its earliest time. It is calculated using the following formula: Total float = Latest finish − earliest start − duration.

Variance   Any deviation of project work from what was planned. Variance can be around costs, time, performance, or project scope.

Work Breakdown Structure (WBS)   A deliverables-oriented "family tree" of project components (products or services) that shows the total scope of the project. Each descending level represents an increasingly detailed definition of a project component. WBS is a methodology that leads to definitions of the hierarchical breakdown of responsibilities and work in a project. Once implemented, the WBS facilitates summary reporting at a variety of levels.

Work Flow   The relationship of the activities in a project from start to finish. Work flow takes into consideration all types of activity relationships.

Work Load   The number of work units assigned to a resource over a period of time.

Work Package   The smallest unit shown in a work breakdown structure chart.

Work Units   A measurement of effort expended by resources. For example, people as a resource can be measured by the number of hours they work.

Zero Float   A condition where there is no excess time between activities. An activity with zero float is considered a critical activity. If the duration of any critical activity is increased (the activity slips), the project finish date will slip.

Summary of Key Project Manager Actions and Results

The following table presents a summary of the major actions that should be taken by project managers to execute a project successfully. For each action, there is a list of one or more results that should be achieved by the action.

You may use this summary to help orient yourself to where you are in the overall project management process or as an aid for developing your daily list of "to-dos."

Action	Results of Successful Performance
Initiating	
1. Demonstrate Project Need and Feasibility	■ A document confirming that there is a need for the project deliverables and describing, in broad terms: the deliverables, means of creating the deliverables, costs of creating and implementing the deliverables, benefits to be obtained by implementing the deliverables.
2. Obtain Project Authorization	■ A go/no go decision is made by the sponsor. ■ A project manager is assigned. ■ A project charter is created that: 　■ Formally recognizes the project 　■ Is issued by a manager external to the project and at a high enough organizational level so that he or she can meet project needs 　■ Authorizes the project manager to apply resources to project activities
3. Obtain Authorization for the Phase	■ A go/no go decision is made by the sponsor that authorizes the project manager to apply organizational resources to the activities of a particular phase.

151

Action	*Results of Successful Performance*
	■ Written approval of the phase is created that: ■ Formally recognizes the existence of the phase ■ Is issued by a manager external to the project and at a high enough organizational level so that he or she can meet project needs
Planning	
4. Describe Project Scope	■ Statement of project scope ■ Scope management plan ■ Work breakdown structure
5. Define and Sequence Project Activities	■ An activity list (list of all activities that will be performed on the project) ■ Updates to the work breakdown structure (WBS) ■ A project network diagram
6. Estimate Durations for Activities and Resources Required	■ Estimate of durations (time required) for each activity and assumptions related to each estimate ■ Statement of resource requirements ■ Updates to activity list
7. Develop a Project Schedule	■ Project schedule in the form of Gantt charts, network diagrams, milestone charts, or text tables ■ Supporting details, such as resource usage over time, cash flow projections, order/delivery schedules
8. Estimate Costs	■ Cost estimates for completing each activity ■ Supporting detail, including assumptions and constraints ■ Cost management plan describing how cost variances will be handled
9. Build a Budget and Spending Plan	■ A cost baseline or time-phased budget for measuring and monitoring costs ■ A spending plan, telling how much will be spent on what resources at what time
10. (Optional) Create a Formal Quality Plan	■ Quality management plan, including operational definitions ■ Quality verification checklists
11. (Optional) Create a Formal Project Communications Plan	■ A communication management plan, including: ■ Collection structure ■ Distribution structure ■ Description of information to be disseminated ■ Schedules listing when information will be produced ■ A method for updating the communications plan
12. Organize and Acquire Staff	■ Role and responsibility assignments ■ Staffing plan ■ Organizational chart with detail as appropriate ■ Project staff ■ Project team directory

Action	Results of Successful Performance
13. (Optional) Identify Risks and Plan to Respond	■ A document describing potential risks, including their sources, symptoms, and ways to address them
14. (Optional) Plan for and Acquire Outside Resources	■ Procurement management plan describing how contractors will be obtained ■ Statement of work (SOW) or statement of requirements (SOR) describing the item (product or service) to be procured ■ Bid documents, such as RFP (request for proposal), IFB (invitation for bid) ■ Evaluation criteria—means of scoring contractor's proposals ■ Contract with one or more suppliers of goods or services
15. Organize the Project Plan	■ A comprehensive project plan that pulls together all the outputs of the preceding project planning activities
16. Close Out the Project Planning Phase	■ A project plan that has been approved, in writing, by the sponsor ■ A green light or okay to begin work on the project
17. Revisit the Project Plan and Replan If Needed	■ Confidence that the detailed plans to execute a particular phase are still accurate and will effectively achieve results as planned
Executing	
18. Execute Project Activities	■ Work results (deliverables) are created. ■ Change requests (i.e., based on expanded or contracted project) are identified. ■ Periodic progress reports are created. ■ Team performance is assessed, guided, and improved if needed. ■ Bids or proposals for deliverables are solicited, contractors (suppliers) are chosen, and contracts are established. ■ Contracts are administered to achieve desired work results.
Controlling	
19. Control Project Activities	■ Decision to accept inspected deliverables ■ Corrective actions such as rework of deliverables, adjustments to work process ■ Updates to project plan and scope ■ List of lessons learned ■ Improved quality ■ Completed evaluation checklists (if applicable)
Closing	
20. Close Out Project Activities	■ Formal acceptance, documented in writing, that the sponsor has accepted the product of this phase or activity ■ Formal acceptance of contractor work products and updates to the contractor's files ■ Updated project records prepared for archiving ■ A plan for follow-up and/or hand-off of work products

```
                    ┌──────────────┐
                    │  APPENDIX D  │
                    └──────┬───────┘
                           │
                           │    POTENTIAL
                           │    SHORTCUTS FOR
                           │    LOW-RISK
                           │    PROJECTS
```

Appendix C: Summary of Key Project Manager Actions and Results identifies a set of specific actions that project managers should take to help ensure the success of their projects. These actions provide certain checks and balances that are essential, especially if the project is complicated, controversial, highly visible, or managed by an inexperienced team. However, there are certain circumstances when fewer safeguards may be needed. For example, if you are both the project manager and the sponsor, it may not be necessary to build in sponsor approvals in your project plans. Or if you are managing a project that is relatively small, employs time-tested processes that have become a matter of routine for your project team, and will lead to the deliverables whose need and feasibility are assured, you may be able to skip or abbreviate several of the key project manager actions.

The table below shows how you might eliminate or abbreviate some of these actions under certain circumstances. Here's what the symbols mean:

- ●   The action should be fully completed.
- ○   The action might be abbreviated.
- —   You might completely skip the action.

155

Action	Low-Risk Example 1: —The project is needed and feasible. —You are your own project sponsor.	Low-Risk Example 2: —The project is needed and feasible. —The project is small and routine. —The project employs time-tested activities.
Initiating		
1. Demonstrate Project Need and Feasibility	—	—
2. Obtain Project Authorization	—	○
3. Obtain Authorization for the Phase	—	○
Planning		
4. Describe Project Scope	○	○
5. Define and Sequence Project Activities	●	○
6. Estimate Durations for Activities and Resources Required	●	○
7. Develop a Project Schedule	●	●
8. Estimate Costs	●	●
9. Build a Budget and Spending Plan	●	●
10. (Optional) Create a Formal Quality Plan	—	—
11. (Optional) Create a Formal Project Communications Plan	—	—
12. Organize and Acquire Staff	○	○
13. (Optional) Identify Risks and Plan to Respond	—	—
14. (Optional) Plan for and Acquire Outside Resources	—	—
15. Organize the Project Plan	○	●
16. Close Out the Project Planning Phase	—	●
17. Revisit the Project Plan and Replan if Needed	●	●
Executing		
18. Execute Project Activities	●	●

Action	Low-Risk Example 1: —The project is needed and feasible. —You are your own project sponsor.	Low-Risk Example 2: —The project is needed and feasible. —The project is small and routine. —The project employs time-tested activities.
Controlling		
19. Control Project Activities	●	●
Closing		
20. Close Out Project Activities	○	●

GUIDELINES FOR DECIDING WHEN TO KILL THE PROJECT

A project often develops enormous momentum as team members devote large amounts of time and energy and even make substantial personal sacrifices (overtime, changes in personal plans, etc.) on behalf of the project. Yet there are some circumstances in which it simply doesn't make sense to continue—in other words, there are times when a project should either be abandoned completely or stopped, reviewed, and then completely replanned from scratch.

Here are some of the circumstances under which it might make sense to abandon the project:

- ■ **_When It No Longer Has Strategic Value._** When the project is no longer contributing to the organization's long- or short-term business strategies, no matter how wonderful the project's end product or process, it should probably be abandoned. Why consume resources for a nonstrategic set of deliverables? Many project managers would say that this is the single most painful situation they face. It's tough to let go—especially when you're building a good product on time and within budget and you've invested a lot of yourself in the project. On the other hand, in today's lightning-fast business world, top managers must frequently abandon business strategies that aren't working or are no longer competitive—and this means directing subordinates to let go of projects that no longer make good business sense.

- ■ **_When It Is Simply No Longer Feasible._** When the project cannot be done properly with the available resources or under the current circumstances, it may make sense to abandon it.

- ■ **_When Deliverables Repeatedly Fail to Appear, Despite the Best Efforts of the Team._** If at first (and second, and third, and fourth!) you don't succeed, you should probably abandon your plan and start from scratch before wasting more resources.

▪ *When the Deliverables Are Substantially and Continually behind Schedule.* In this circumstance, you should first try to adjust the scope, apply more resources, or adjust the quality level. If these fail, then the plan is likely bad and should be abandoned.

▪ *When There Are More Issues Than Successes.* Call them problems, concerns, or plain old troubles, but when issues outnumber the successfully completed milestones and deliverables, you probably have a poorly designed project. The project should probably be abandoned and stakeholders (especially the issue-defining stakeholders) reassembled to design a new project from scratch—one that accommodates the issues.

▪ *When Budget or Resource Allocations Are Continually Exceeded.* This probably means a poor project design, including inadequate scope description, poor estimate of resources, and inadequate cost estimate. Consider rethinking the entire project and starting again with a more reasonable budget or resource allocation. If these can't be obtained, then reduce the deliverables, either in quality or quantity, so that they more realistically match the available resources and funds.

```
┌─────────────┐
│  APPENDIX F │
└──────┬──────┘
       │
```

TAKING CHARGE OF YOUR PROJECT MANAGEMENT SOFTWARE

Your project management software is like a Swiss Army knife. It can do a lot of things for you, but there are probably only a few things that you actually need it to do. As a novice user, you can waste hours in front of your computer clicking on icons and rummaging through pull-down menus. That's fine if your purpose is to explore the software. However, if you need to create a project plan quickly, it's better to make some notes and get organized before you switch on your system.

Follow these steps to take charge of your project management software.

Step 1: Make sure you do your homework regarding your project's authorization and scope. Refer to these Action Items and complete all of the pertinent worksheets:

- Demonstrate Project Need and Feasibility
- Obtain Project Authorization
- Describe Project Scope

The point: Don't spend time trying to use your software to plan a project that hasn't been authorized or adequately scoped.

Step 2: Start to define and sequence, in rough paper-and-pencil form, your project's activities, and assemble any data you have (rules of thumb, organization history, etc.) regarding durations for typical project activities. In particular, try to find sample project schedules to use as a model and look for task relationships (which tasks must come before and which must come after certain activities). Also, try to figure out which project activities can be completed in parallel (at the same time). Refer to these Action Items and examine all of the pertinent worksheets:

- Define and Sequence Project Activities
- Estimate Durations for Activities and Resources Required
- Develop a Project Schedule
- Estimate Costs
- Build a Budget and Spending Plan

The point: By reviewing these Action Items you will be able to form a mental picture of the kinds of outputs that you want from your project management software. This way you will be prepared to drive the software instead of letting the software drive you.

Step 3: Set realistic expectations about using the software. Consider these benefits and limitations:

Benefits: Project management software can help you:

- Plan faster and more accurately using templates (disk-based copies of former project plans).
- Compare alternatives quickly and easily by allowing you to make changes and see the results.
- Avoid overbooking people, equipment, and facilities by identifying resource overallocations.
- Find the critical path easily and shorten it.
- Communicate your plans through top-quality schedules and reports.
- Customize project schedules and reports for particular individuals.
- Update plans more often and more accurately.
- Respond to crises with a solid project database behind you. Instead of shooting from the hip, you can quickly create alternate scenarios that can be evaluated in detail by the sponsor and stakeholders

Limitations: Project management software cannot:

- Define your project goals, objectives, or scope.
- Decide who's best for doing a particular job.
- Decide how to do the job.
- Estimate time typically required for completing a particular task. You'll need to ask experts!
- Reallocate overbooked resources.
- Figure out how to fix schedule slips.
- *Think for you!*

Step 4: Decide exactly what you want from the software and then go after it. And don't allow yourself to be intimidated by an overabundance of menus and choices that you don't understand. (After all, do you really understand all the options that your word processing software makes available? Probably not! You simply ignore the menus and options that you don't need to use. So give yourself permission to ignore some of the menus and options available in your PM software!)

The table below can help you stay focused on particular chores that you want the software to perform. Here's how it works: Use the "IF . . ." column to figure out what you want the software to do for you; then place a check mark (✓) beside each item. Later, you can refer to the "THEN . . ." column to help you identify terms to look for in the software documentation, help screens, menus, and so on.

✓	*IF you want the software to help you do this:*	*THEN look for information on these terms on menus, help screens, and in documentation:*
	Make an outlined list of project tasks	Enter tasks, schedule tasks, outlining, insert tasks
	Figure out how the tasks are related (which are prerequisite to others, which overlap, etc.)	Link tasks, task relationships, Gantt chart, PERT chart, lead vs. lag time
	Create a schedule from the outlined task list	Project start date, task durations
	Keep a list of resources (people, equipment, facilities) and the cost of each (hourly rate, one-time fees, etc.)	Resources, resource list, resource cost
	Assign specific resources to specific tasks	Resource allocation, resource assignment, task assignment
	Set up unique calendars for each resource that show workdays and days off	Calendar, project calendar, resource calendar, work days, holidays
	Balance the workload so that no resources are asked to do too many tasks at once	Leveling (manual), leveling (automatic), resource allocation/assignment
	Figure out how much each task will cost to complete, given the resources assigned to it	Resource rates, fixed costs, variable costs, cost accrual, total cost per task, total cost per project
	At any point in time, compare the actual project status to the scheduled project status	Project baseline, tracking progress, updating tasks, updating schedule, variance (cost, schedule, work)
	Figure out how to reduce the time required	Critical path (analyzing and reducing), optimizing schedule, reducing project time
	Figure out how to reduce the cost	Cost reduction, cash flow, controlling costs
	Communicate general project information to managers, sponsors, and the internal project team using professional quality schedules and reports	Reports, printing, Gantt chart, PERT chart, calendar, task report, cost report, resource report, enhancing reports, worksheets, status report, workload report, custom report
	Customize schedules and reports to meet particular needs of the recipient (management overview, schedule for one resource only, cost of one phase, etc.)	[See all of preceding] Customizing reports, filtering, selecting data for reports

✓	*IF you want the software to help you do this:*	*THEN look for information on these terms on menus, help screens, and in documentation:*
	Do all the above for multiple projects at the same time	Multiple projects, consolidate projects, subprojects, link projects
	Make a new project plan from existing project data	Templates, resource pool, master calendar, change defaults

Step 5: Start up your computer, activate your PM software, and enter project data by completing these substeps:

A. Refer to the preceding checklist.

B. Go to the first checked item on the list.

C. Refer to your notes about the project; then use the software to perform this item. When you get stuck, look for help by using the suggested terms to search through help screens, on-line coaches, or software documentation.

D. When you feel you have completed the item, go on to your next checked item (substep B) and repeat the process using substeps C and D.

```
┌─────────────┐
│ APPENDIX G  │
└──────┬──────┘
       │
```

SELECTED PROJECT MANAGER RESOURCES

This Appendix provides information about PM-oriented web sites and PM-oriented publications.

PM-Oriented Internet Sites

Below is a list of web sites which the reader of this book will likely find valuable. Please note that this is not intended to be a comprehensive list—simply a starting point for the PM-focused web surfer. Nearly all of these sites provide links to other PM-oriented web sites, so any one of them is a good place to start your Internet search.

Michael Greer's Project Management Resources: www.michaelgreer.com. This web site, which I created and maintain, provides the following:

- Free PM-oriented handouts from my public speaking engagements
- A frequently updated bibliography of PM books, as well as hot links to on-line articles
- A list of my public speaking engagements
- Links to other PM-oriented web sites
- Information about my customizable on-site workshops, including the popular two-day, hands-on session, *Project Management Basics*
- Free information about my work in instructional development PM, including downloadable tools and handouts for those trying to plan and manage the development of training materials
- Tables of contents for all of my books
- Announcements about my new publications

AllPM.com: http://allpm.com/. "The internet's premier site for Information Technology (IT) project management information and resources." It includes discussion groups, links to articles, links to PM-oriented web sites, and much more.

Free Management Library: http://www.mapnp.org/library/. This site is devoted to all sorts of management topics, many of which relate to nonprofit organizations. In its own words, "This library is a community resource to be shared and contributed to by the public. The overall goal of the library is to provide basic, how-to management information to managers—particularly those with very limited resources."

The Project Management Forum: http://www.pmforum.org/. "The Project Management Forum is a non-profit resource for information on international project management affairs dedicated to development, international cooperation, promotion and support of a professional and worldwide project management discipline."

The Project Management Institute: http://www.pmi.org. "PMI establishes Project Management standards, provides seminars, educational programs and professional certification." Visitors can download a free copy of *A Guide to the Project Management Body of Knowledge* from this site.

The Project Management Institute Online Bookstore: http://www.pmibookstore.org/. "PMI Bookstore is your online access to the most complete collection of project management information in the world. Whether you know the title you're looking for or if you just want to browse, the PMI Bookstore is the place to find . . . more than 1,000 of the best project management books in print."

Projectworld: http://www.projectworld.com/. The ProjectWorld web site provides information about the semiannual ProjectWorld conferences and exhibitions held alternately in the eastern and western United States.

An Idiosyncratic Bibliography

An idiosyncratic mixture of some of my favorite references relating to project management (PM); project management software; the management of instructional development (ID) projects; and the broad topics of instructional development (ID), training, mentoring, and Human Performance Technology (HPT) is available at **www.michaelgreer.com**; I update it every couple of weeks.

Notes

Introduction

  1. The Project Management Institute, *A Guide to the Project Management Body of Knowledge (PMBOK)* (Upper Darby, PA: PMI, 1994), p. 20.

  2. Ibid., pp. 2–3, 63.

  3. Ibid., pp. 4, 63.

  4. Ibid., p. 4.

  5. Ibid.

  6. Ibid., p. 63.

  7. Ibid., p. 5.

  8. Ibid., p. 8.

  9. Ibid.

10. Ibid.

11. Ibid.

12. Ibid., pp. 8–9.

13. Ibid.

14. Ibid., p. 10.

15. Ibid., pp. 10–11.

Part I

  1. Ibid., p. 2.

  2. Ibid., pp. 6, 62.

  3. Ibid., p. 64.

  4. Ibid., pp. 6–7, 63.

  5. Ibid., p. 63.

  6. Ibid., pp. 7–8, 64.

  7. Ibid., pp. 6–8, 20.

  8. Ibid., pp. 6–8, 13–14.

  9. Ibid., pp. 6–8.

10. Ibid.
11. Ibid.

Part II

 1. Ibid., p. 13.
 2. Ibid., p. 12.
 3. Ibid.
 4. Ibid.
 5. Ibid., pp 12–13.
 6. Ibid., p. 13.
 7. Ibid., pp. 13–14.
 8. Ibid., pp. 14–15.
 9. Ibid., p. 15.
10. Ibid., pp. 15, 61.
11. Ibid., p. 15.
12. Ibid., p. 16.

Part III

 1. Ibid.
 2. Ibid., p. 20.
 3. Ibid., p. 21.
 4. Ibid.
 5. Ibid.
 6. Ibid.
 7. Ibid.
 8. Ibid.
 9. Ibid.
10. Ibid.
11. Ibid., pp. 22, 64.
12. Ibid., p. 22.
13. Ibid.
14. Ibid., p. 21.
15. Ibid.
16. Ibid., p. 24.
17. Ibid., p. 25.
18. Ibid.
19. Ibid.
20. Ibid.

21. Ibid., p. 26.
22. Ibid., p. 31.
23. Ibid.
24. Ibid., p. 26.
25. Ibid.
26. Ibid.
27. Ibid., p. 28.
28. Ibid., p. 29.
29. Ibid.
30. Ibid., p. 27.
31. Ibid.
32. Ibid., p. 31.
33. Ibid.
34. Ibid.
35. Ibid.
36. Ibid., p. 32.
37. Ibid., p. 31.
38. Ibid., p. 32.
39. Ibid., p. 35.
40. Ibid.
41. Ibid., pp. 35–36.
42. Ibid., p. 35.
43. Ibid., pp. 36, 64.
44. Ibid., p. 64.
45. Ibid., p. 35.
46. Ibid., p. 43.
47. Ibid., p. 42.
48. Ibid.
49. Ibid., p. 43.
50. Ibid., pp. 39–40.
51. Ibid., p. 38.
52. Ibid., p. 40.
53. Ibid., p. 38.
54. Ibid., pp. 38–39.
55. Ibid., p. 40.
56. Ibid., p. 39.
57. Ibid.
58. Ibid., p. 40.
59. Ibid., pp. 46–48.
60. Ibid., p. 45.
61. Ibid.
62. Ibid., p. 46.
63. Ibid.

64. Ibid., p. 47.
65. Ibid., p. 46.
66. Ibid., p. 47.
67. Ibid., pp 46–47.
68. Ibid., pp 51–53.
69. Ibid., p. 50.
70. Ibid.
71. Ibid., p. 51.
72. Ibid.
73. Ibid., p. 52.
74. Ibid.
75. Ibid.
76. Ibid., p. 51.
77. Ibid., pp. 51–52.
78. Ibid., p. 52.
79. Ibid., p. 53.
80. Ibid., p. 17.
81. Ibid., pp. 18, 63.
82. Ibid., pp. 17–19.
83. Ibid.
84. Ibid., pp. 43–44.
85. Ibid., pp. 40–41.
86. Ibid., pp. 52–53.
87. Ibid., pp. 53–54.
88. Ibid., p. 15.
89. Ibid., p. 23.
90. Ibid., p. 44.
91. Ibid., p. 54.
92. Ibid., p. 23.
93. Ibid., p. 54.
94. Ibid., p. 44.
95. Ibid., p. 54.
96. Ibid., p. 44.

Index

Activities
    and dependencies, 49–50
    close-out of, 129
    defining of, 49–50, 141
    duration estimates for, 55, 58
    sequencing of, 50–53
administrative closure, 23, 129
alternatives, identification of, 48
analogous estimating, 70
application area, practice of, 3
arrow diagramming method (ADM), 53

bar chart
    as scheduling tool, 62
    defined, 144
benchmarking, 78
benefit-cost analysis, 48
best practices, 3, 12
bottom-up cost estimates, 70, 72–73
budget
    guidelines for building, 75–77
    time-phased, 75

calendar, 63
    defined, 139
    sample, 66
cause-and-effect diagram, 78
change control, 22
closing out, defined, 142
closing process, 23
    action item for, 30
    subprocesses of, 129
communications
    planning, 81–84

    use of e-mail in, 84
conditional diagramming method, 53
contract administration, 22
contract close-out, 23, 129
contractors
    contract negotiations with, 101
    evaluation of, 99
    selection guidelines for, 100–101
control, defined, 142
controlling process, 22
    action item for, 30
    and variances, 117, 118
    procedures, 118
    subprocesses of, 117
core team, value of, 34
cost, vs. price, 70
cost control, 22
cost estimates
    accuracy of, 71
    bottom-up, 72–73
    guidelines for, 72–73
    methods of, 70
    techniques for, 73
    worksheet for, 72
crashing, 68

decomposition, 43
deliverables
    creation of, 15, 17
    defined, 9, 142
    finished, 9, 44
    implementation of, 16, 17
    interim, 9, 44
    review questions, 133–134

deliverables (*continued*)
    sign-off of, 121
    specifications for, 14, 17
    status review of, 120, 122
    testing of, 16, 17
    vs. goals, 10
dependencies, types of, 49–50
design of experiments technique, 80
discretionary dependencies, 50
discretionary planning, 21
duration
    assumptions about, 61
    defined, 143
    estimates, 55–60
    resource-based, 148
    vs. effort, 55–56
    vs. resources, 59–60
duration compression, 68, 143

e-mail, inefficient use of, 84
Economy, Peter, 114
effort
    vs. duration, 55–56
    vs. resources, 59–60
Effort/Duration table, 56, 57
essential planning, 21
executing process, 22, 143
    action item for, 30
experts, *see* subject-area experts
external dependencies, 50

fast-tracking, 68
feasibility determination, 12, 16, 31–33
finished deliverables, 9
fishbone diagram, 78
fixed budget estimating, 70
fixed-cost resources, 71
flowcharts, 78
functional organization, 5, 144

Gantt chart, as scheduling tool, 62, 144
general management
    defined, 3
    skills, 6
Generic Project Life Cycle, 12, 13
    phases of, 12–15

goals
    defined, 144
    vs. deliverables, 10
graphical evaluation and review technique
    (GERT), 53

information distribution, 22
initiating process, 20, 144
    action items for, 30
interim deliverables, 9
International Organization for Standards
    (ISO), 79
Internet sites, for project management,
    165–166
invitation for bid (IFB), 96, 98
Ishikawa diagram, 78

kickoff meetings, 113

lag time, 50, 145
lead time, 50, 145
loops, 53

management skills
    general, 6
    ongoing enterprise, 6
mandatory dependencies, 49–50
mathematical analysis, 68
matrix organization, 6, 145
milestone chart
    as scheduling tool, 63
    sample, 66
milestone, defined, 11, 145
My Unique Project Life Cycle worksheet,
    16–17

need demonstration, 12, 16, 31–33
Nelson, Bob, 114
network diagram, 50–52
    as scheduling tool, 62, 64, 65
    defined, 146
network templates, 53

ongoing operations
    defined, 146
    vs. programs and projects, 2

optimization methods, 33
organization
   functional, 5
   matrix, 6
   projectized, 5–6
organizational planning, 85–86
organizational structures, types of, 4–6

parametric modeling, 74
phases, *see* project phases
planning
   action items for, 42
   discretionary, 21
   essential, 21
planning process, 20–21
   action items for, 30
postmortem, 131
postproject review, 131
precedence diagramming method (PDM), 53
price, vs. cost, 70
process
   defined, 19
   types of, 19–20
procurement
   defined, 96
   management plan, 96
   planning, 97–99
product analysis, 48
programs
   defined, 2–3, 146
   vs. ongoing operations, 2–3
progress reporting, 22
project
   authorization of, 35–38, 39–41
   charter, 35, 147
   compared to industry standards, 12
   cost estimating for, 70–74
   defined, 2, 9, 147
   deliverables, *see* deliverables
   evaluation, 120
   feasibility determination for, 12, 16, 31–33
   formal approval of, 35, 39
   guidelines for abandoning, 159–160
   hand-off, 131
   influence of organizational structures on,
     4–6

   life cycle of, *see* project life cycle
   need determination for, 12, 16, 31–33
   phases, *see* project phases
   responsibility/accountability matrix for, 88
   sign-off, 131, 134–135
   staffing for, 85–86
   vs. ongoing operations, 2–3
   vs. programs, 1
   vs. subprojects, 3–4
   written approval of, 38, 41
Project Charter worksheet, 36–37
project communications plan
   creation of, 81–82
   worksheet for, 83
Project Communications Planner, 83
Project Deliverables' Status Analyzer work-
    sheet, 122
Project Issue Tracker worksheet, 126
project life cycle
   defined, 11
   phases of, 12–15
project management
   and risk assessment, 94
   as a profession, 1
   checklist, 120–121
   closing process, 23
   controlling process, 22
   defined, 3, 145
   executing process, 22
   initiating process, 20
   Internet sites for, 165–166
   key actions, 151–154
     shortcuts for, 155–157
     worksheet, 24–27
   planning process, 20
project management processes, 19–23
   vs. project phases, 23–24, 27–28
project management software
   and "what if" analysis, 128
   benefits of, 162
   defined, 145
   Internet sites, 165–166
   limitations of, 162
   option checklist, 163–164
   use for cost estimating, 74
   use for network diagrams, 53

project management software (*continued*)
  use for scheduling, 63, 68–69
project manager
  and clarification of project scope, 48
  and creation of duration estimate, 60
  and sequencing of activities, 53
  as stakeholder, 12
  cost estimating by, 73–74, 77
  feasibility assessment by, 33
  key actions, 151–154
    shortcuts for, 155–157
    worksheet, 24–27
  scheduling by, 68
project network diagram, 50–52
project phases, 10–11
  and project management processes, 23–
    24, 27–28
  close-out of, 130–131, 159–160
  defined, 147
  execution of, 111–115
  guidelines for controlling, 119–120
project plan
  approval of, 105–106
  creation of, 13–14, 16
  defined, 145
  execution of, 22
  organization of, 102–103
  revisit of, 108–109
project schedule
  as communication tool, 69
  defined, 148
  development of, 62
  guidelines for, 63, 67–68
  selecting format for, 63
project scope, 42
  change, *see* project scope change
  checklist, 45
  defined, 148
  statement, 47
  verification, 23, 129
  weekly review of, 120
project scope change
  defined, 124, 149
  management of, 22, 124
  review of, 121, 124, 125
Project Scope Change Order worksheet, 125

Project Scope Statement worksheet, 47
Project Sign-Off form, 134–135
Project Status Report worksheet, 127
project status review, 121, 127
project team members
  defined, 148
  development of, 22
  recognizing contributions of, 114–115
projectized organization, 5–6, 148

quality assurance, 22
quality control, 22
quality plan, creation of, 78–80
quality policy, 78

recruiting, *see* staff acquisition
replanning, 108–109
request for proposal (RFP), 96, 98
resource leveling, 68, 148
resources
  assumptions about, 61
  defined, 55, 148
  fixed-cost, 71
  make vs. buy decision, 98
  outside, acquisition of, *see* procurement
  requirement estimates for, 58
  requirement statement, 55
  variable-cost, 71
responsibility/accountability matrix, 88
risk
  defined, 91
  identification, 91, 92, 94
  quantification, 91, 92–93
  response options, 93
Risk Assessment and Response Analyzer,
    93–94
risk control, 22
risk management plan, 93

schedule, *see* project schedule
scope, *see* project scope
simulation, 68
solicitation, 22
  defined, 97
  guidelines for, 99
  planning, 97

source selection, 22, 97
spending plan, 75–77
spreadsheet software, use of for cost estimating, 74
staff acquisition
   organizational plan for, 85–86
   pitfalls in, 89
   strategy for, 86–88
stakeholders
   agreement on assumptions, 34
   authorization by, 39
   defined, 149
   early involvement of, 104
   seeking support among, 37
   types of, 11–12
statement of requirements (SOR), 96, 98
statement of work (SOW), 96, 98, 147
subject-matter experts
   defined, 149
   enlisting support from, 48, 53

used for duration estimates, 60
used for scheduling, 68
working with, 137–139
subprojects, defined, 3–4, 149

team members, *see* project team members
text table
   as scheduling tool, 63
   sample, 66

variable-cost resources, 71
Variance Analyzer worksheet, 123
variances, 22, 117, 118
   analysis of, 121, 123
   defined, 150
vendor, *see* contractor

work breakdown structure (WBS), 14, 43, 44, 45
   defined, 150

7755

ABOUT THE AUTHOR

Michael Greer is the author of the first edition of *The Project Manager's Partner: A Step-by-Step Guide to Project Management* (HRD Press, 1996), as well as the facilitator's guide, *Project Management for Workgroups* (HRD Press, 1997). In addition, Greer wrote *The Manager's Pocket Guide to Project Management* (HRD Press, 1999) and the award-winning *ID Project Management: Tools and Techniques for Instructional Designers and Developers* (Educational Technology Publications, 1992). For many years Greer managed teams of contractors as they worked side by side with new product developers to create training and performance improvement systems for major corporations. In his role as consultant and PM workshop administrator, Greer has helped many organizations redesign their PM practices. His primary mission is to demystify PM and make it accessible to new and part-time project managers.

For free handouts, a frequently updated PM bibliography, links to PM-related web sites, and other PM information, visit Michael Greer's Project Management Resources web site at: **www.michaelgreer.com.**

For assistance customizing Greer's HRD Press materials for your organization or to schedule a custom-tailored, in-house PM workshop, contact:

Michael Greer
Voice: (310) 397-0097 (winter/spring)
Voice: (814) 797-2846 (summer/fall)
Voice Mail: (530) 688-6613
Fax: (508) 256-8927
e-mail: INFO@michaelgreer.com